WHAT HAPPENED ALONG THE WAY

A Memoir | 1948-2018

DAN ROTT

Cover and book design by
Amy Livingstone, Sacred Art Studio
sacredartstudio.net

ISBN: 9798655687066

CONTENTS

PART ONE: Growing Up in the Twentieth Century *1*

1. *The Riveter and Mom to the Rescue* *2*
2. *The Ten Foot Hit* *5*
3. *The Soda Fountain Treat* *8*
4. *The Unexpected Gift* *11*
5. *The Accordion Band* *14*
6. *The Toxic DDT Fog* *17*
7. *The Nut Pickers of Dixon* *20*
8. *The One-Room Dakota Schoolhouse* *23*
9. *The Visit to Meet Grandma Johnson* *26*
10. *The Local Butler* *30*
11. *The Dance Card* *33*
12. *The Hunting Accident* *36*
13. *The Mexico Trip: Part One* *40*
14. *The Mexico Trip: Part Two* *44*
15. *The Barnyard Fight* *48*
16. *The Day the Crushers Rode into Town* *51*
17. *The End of the Season* *55*
18. *The Trip to Chico State* *58*
19. *The Last Time I Saw Darryl* *61*

PART TWO: College Years *65*

20. *The Actor and Me* *66*
21. *The Summer Job Prank* *69*
22. *The Dixon Watering Hole* *73*
23. *The Big Downtown Bust* *76*
24. *The Night the Street Clapped* *79*
25. *The Running of the Bulls* *83*
26. *The Unsuspecting Escort* *87*

PART THREE: Career and Family *91*

27. *The POW Teacher* *92*

28. *The Snow Day* *95*

29. *The Life Saving Squeeze* *98*

30. *The Poisonous Smell* *101*

31. *The Team Honor* *105*

32. *The Worst Proposal Ever* *108*

33. *The Lung Collapse* *110*

34. *The Parachute Ride* *113*

35. *The Trail Ride* *116*

36. *The Conference from Hell* *120*

37. *The Shocking Crash* *123*

38. *The Agate Hunters* *127*

39. *The Beginning of the End* *130*

40. *The House Fire* *133*

41. *The Parent Murder* *136*

42. *The Number 24 Tram* *140*

43. *The Sudden Attack* *143*

44. *The Weird Sniff Hotel* *147*

45. *The Return to Hunspach* *149*

46. *The Saddest Clouds* *153*

ON MEMOIRS

Perhaps this is an exercise of self-affirmation, that one's existence has been worthwhile and possibly even memorable. Or does it have a higher purpose, to fill gaps for future generations who, one hopes, might care or even enjoy it? Then again, maybe it is only desire to explain to one's children just why one is the way one is. It might even be interesting for them to identify characteristics in themselves they may have inherited.

—Lisa Ward

… sometimes remembering will lead to a story, which makes it forever. That's what stories are for. Stories are for joining the past to the future. Stories are for those late hours in the night when you can't remember how you got from where you were to where you are. Stories are for eternity, when memory is erased, when there is nothing to remember except the story.

—Tim O'Brien, *The Things They Carried*

…These are true stories told from memory, to which you are entitled to ask, what is the truth? Was there ever such a thing as a pure memory? I doubt it. Even when we convince ourselves that we're being dispassionate, sticking to the bald facts with no self-serving decorations or omissions, pure memory remains as elusive as a bar of wet soap…

—John Le Carré, *The Pigeon Tunnel*

I am bound to
them, though I cannot
look into their eyes or
hear their voices.
I honor their history.
I cherish their lives.
I will tell their story.
I will remember them.

—An old German proverb

To the best of my knowledge, my stories are real events.
The conversations are reconstructed to move the stories along.
I badly wanted to tell about what occurred in small-town culture
as it existed in California with my family in the 20th century. I was
too young or not born yet to have participated in every event, but I
do remember stories told to me. Some names were changed in the
interest of privacy.

—Daniel Rott

DEDICATION

I dedicate this book to my family: past, present and future. When my children Erik, Tara, and Ivan were still at home, I began thinking of stories told to me by my grandfather, my father, and my mother about their lives while growing up. As I started asking questions, the time ran out to learn as much as I wanted to know from them. There was so much more to know about how they lived and what life was like when they were young. What a loss! They grew up when their immigrant families homesteaded land and built lives in a new world. Stories of the old country, emigration, the Great Depression, a huge world war, and having children of their own are largely lost. I hope my children and grandchildren like these simple stories of my life growing up in small-town America and cherish them as I do. Maybe someday, they too will choose to write their own stories for our family to share with those coming after we are gone. This includes, of course, Hattie, Zinnia, Casey, and Grady.

ACKNOWLEDGEMENTS

I wish to thank my writing family from the memoirs class I attended for the past several years. With their encouragement and writing samples, my writing skills improved and grew from each class and year. I started the program with few skills and no knowledge of what's involved in the art of memoir writing. I especially want to thank my instructors and the Osher Lifelong Learning Institute (OLLI) provided by the University of California at Davis. My first writing teacher, **Marcy Lorfing**, was incredibly patient and helpful no matter how weak my writing assignment. **Kit Kirkpatrick** followed as class teacher with short, concise writing suggestions and samples that proved invaluable. She also encouraged me with her "sighs" at the end of stories I read to the class. Editor Jill Kelly, PhD, provided valuable advice and support in getting this project into a book. Finally, I must note that my wife, **Joan,** encouraged me to start this project.

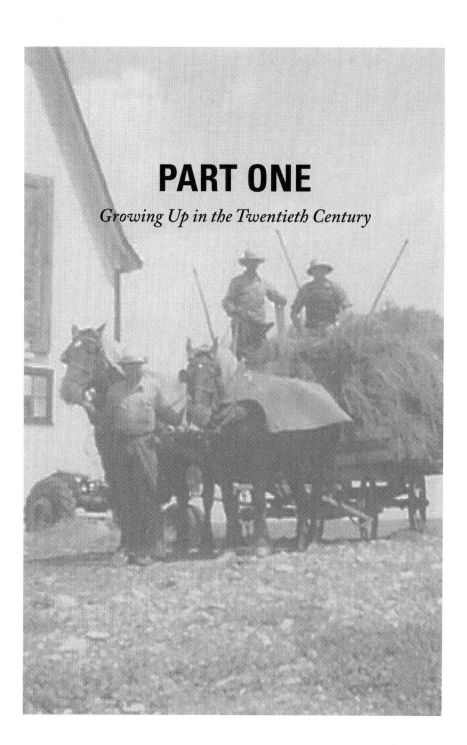

PART ONE

Growing Up in the Twentieth Century

Chapter 1

THE RIVETER AND MOM TO THE RESCUE

I wasn't born yet, but I suspect the conversation began with my mom saying, "Let's get out of this icebox and go to California. The weather is always sunny, there are plenty of men from all over the country and the nightspots are always hopping."

Her friend, Tillie Mortenson, experienced life much like my mom did. She worked hard and struggled to find a good job and a stable place to settle. "I have friends who've made the move. Why not? We're not making any headway here in the Twin Cities and we're already 22. Let's go. I hear there are jobs for women that pay more than we can ever make here. When do we leave?"

Tillie was a thin, golden-haired woman with a lot in common with my mom, except she was reserved and shy by nature. Her parents were immigrants from Denmark and she was a rural girl who had worked a variety of jobs before landing a factory job in Minneapolis, where she met my mom, who had moved there to get a better paying job. She liked my mom's energy and outgoing, open personality, and they liked going out on the town together.

As far as I can tell, my mom left home when she was 15. This is about the same age my grandmother was when she left Norway to come to North America. My mom left Harmony, Minnesota, in the mid-1930s. Her family owned a small dairy in the southeast corner of the state near the Iowa-Wisconsin border. She moved in with relatives who lived in Winona, Minnesota, and she became the live-in baby sitter for her cousin, who had several small children. She never spoke about this transition in her life, maybe because she didn't return to school and never got a high school diploma. Maybe there was more to the story, I don't know.

My grandmother, Ronnaug Saether, arrived first in Canada and married a man named Jens Jensen. The marriage didn't last long enough for my mother's arrival in 1921. Born Borghild Jensen, my mom and Grandma left after a short time for southern Minnesota where more members of the large Saether family had immigrated early in the 20th century. Norway was a poor country at the time and many Norwegians headed to the New World although half of her large family stayed behind in their native land.

Life was hard during the depression years as most Americans struggled to survive the decade leading to World War II. Grandma met and married her second husband, Hellick Johnson in Minnesota, and together they built a small farm and had five more children: Norval, Ruth, Gladys, Harold, and Margaret, who contracted polio at an early age. Mom, being the oldest and a half-sister, shouldered a heavy load of early morning milking, feeding cows, and getting her brothers and sisters ready for school. Life on the dairy meant working seven days a week and part of the night, as well.

My mom and Grandma Johnson were similarly strong-willed. Once their mind was made up, they moved ahead without looking back. It appears that at some point, Mom's needs weren't being met, she and Grandma argued, and she decided to leave home. More moves and transitions occurred before Mom settled in Alameda, California. Tillie and Mom became part of the large contingent of women known as "Rosie the Riveters," whose efforts on behalf of the war effort in building transport ships helped win the war of supply and resupply. They had grown up with hard work and filled in when the need was greatest. I'm as proud of my mom's participation as a "Rosie the Riveter" as I am of my dad's participation in the Navy during the war.

In 1943, Tillie met a young sailor named Emer Rott and they dated briefly before he was deployed to the Aleutian Islands shortly after they met. When he returned a year and a half later, he immediately called Tillie. I suspect the call went something like this: "Tillie, this is Emer. I'm back and can't wait to see you again."

"Emer, I have something to tell you. I met a guy named Bob. We're going to get married, but my roommate, Bea, broke up with her boyfriend. Why don't you call her?"

This was a common occurrence during wartime.

My mom married Emer Rott on February 3, 1945. I was born on July 10, 1948, in Susanville, California, and my story starts here.

Chapter 2

THE TEN FOOT HIT

On June 1, 1955, I was six years and 11 months old, one month short of the minimum age to join the Dixon, California youth baseball program in what was called the Peanut League. America was in love with baseball, and I was determined to be a part of it regardless of age restrictions, but I had to fight to play.

"Get down, Shorty. Crouch! Lower!" yelled voices from the Pirates bench. "Use your knees. Bend your knees." I was at bat in my first game as a member of the Dixon *Pirates*. We were playing another team in Dixon's youth league. The coach and older members of the team had shown me several times how I needed to get low to the ground until I looked like a ground hog hunting for acorns. If the truth were known, I was terrified.

Dixon's program had six teams assembled in a unique arrangement. Since the town was small and the number of kids who wanted to play baseball was also small, the league had players from ages 7 to 12. The more difficult positions like pitcher, catcher, shortstop, and first base were manned by older players. Younger players manned right field because only a few kids hit left-handed. Right field is where the ball travels if it is hit out of the infield by a lefty. In most games, few, if any, balls are hit into right field. Younger players almost never started the game but usually played at the end of the seven innings. But it was a rule that all players had to play at least one inning, which allowed younger kids to slowly develop their knowledge and skills in the highly nuanced game of baseball.

"Ball one," called a black-clad umpire.

At my first time at bat, I started questioning the wisdom of begging my dad to help me play at such an early age. My mind raced back a month to when my dad had taken me down to the park to find Coach Red Finney, the Summer Recreation Program director. Coach Finney was a local community hero and the leader of Dixon sports and athletic programs. A former Marine who had served in the Pacific Island campaigns, Coach Finney had made his reputation in Dixon coaching the high school football teams. His teams had won eight straight football championships. He looked the part: a tough guy with hair cropped close, red stubble on a rugged face with a scar that crossed his left cheek. He habitually wore aviation-style dark glasses, a white t-shirt that fit tightly across his chest and shoulders, athletic shorts or football jersey pants without the pads that stopped short of his knees. I don't think I ever saw him without a lanyard and whistle around his neck. In many settings, the coach looked out of place, but in Dixon, he swaggered around town like a Spartan warrior.

My dad and I tracked down the coach to plead my case: I was ready to play baseball. Several friends in my class who had spring birthdays were being allowed to play since their seventh birthday came before June 1, the formal age needed for summer ball. But my birthday fell on July 10 and I was therefore not eligible.

"He's not old enough, Emer," the coach told my dad, who wouldn't take no for an answer.

After a few minutes, Coach Finney consented but told us in an annoyed but authoritative way, "If he starts, I expect him to finish. I don't like quitters."

We both gave our most determined look and said we understood. I pounded on my new mitt a few times to emphasize my determination. The mitt was almost flat and looked like a dark, rotting starfish, nothing like the beautifully constructed, concaved leather gloves that were developed in the decades to follow, but I still felt like quite the athlete.

"Ball two," shouted the umpire.

"Get down lower, Short Stuff." The air was full of noises and shouts.

I came close to regretting my bravado with the coach. I had just finished first grade and the pitcher was going into junior high and was also one of those kids who matured early. His face was starting to lose its baby cheeks for something a little more leathery.

"Ball three," shouted the umpire.

"Shrink more. Look for clover..." The yelling became more creative.

During that first season of organized baseball, I learned so much. I didn't get lots of playing time but I learned the game in a special way. The older boys taught me things I might not have learned playing with others my own age. After jumping up and down with glee because we scored a winning run, I learned that a *balk*, where all players advance one base, only sounds like *bop*, and that jumping up and down yelling *bop* did not go over well with the baseball crowd. Baseball takes time and a commitment to learn, and being a part of a team of older players who knew through experience how to work together helped my learning process.

Did I get a hit that first time at the plate? No, but I did get a walk, which seemed to make the other members of my team happy and accept me a little. I didn't get my first hit until about three-quarters of the way into the season. I was in my normal crouching position hoping for a walk when a pitcher without accurate control threw a ball that hit my bat, which was settled firmly on my shoulder. The ball plunked down off the bat and rolled for about ten yards. On his way to get to the ball and throw me out, the catcher fell on his bottom and was unable to throw to first base. An error by the catcher? I didn't think so. My senses picked up only howls, yells, and whistles coming from our bench as I stood on first base praying I would know what to do next.

WHAT HAPPENED ALONG THE WAY

Chapter 3

THE SODA FOUNTAIN TREAT

To this day I am mathematically challenged. I used to blame that on my mom because I know she smoked cigarettes when I was a baby. Was I kidding myself? Who knows? but that's why I cringed when Mom said, "How'd your school day go? Did you do any better at math?"

"Okay," I answered most of the time. "I'm having trouble with borrowing and carrying, but Mrs. Holmes says that I am getting better."

When I was 7, I walked home from school almost every day. If the weather was really cold or rainy, I caught a ride with a neighbor. No one thought it out of the ordinary for a second or third grade student to walk home, even if it meant crossing the railroad tracks slicing through town. People of all ages walked to the store or even to work.

Sometimes I stopped at the dental offices where my mom worked to say hi. Once a month I stopped in to ask for some money, which I used to treat myself at the soda fountain of one of Dixon's two drugstores. The soda fountain counter was still in full force, but things were changing quickly. The Soda Fountain looked very much like a traditional bar, but instead of alcoholic beverages, ice cream, milk shakes and sodas of all kinds were sold. Occasionally, various food selections were offered.

"Hi Mom. Can I stop by Gruesendorf's to get a soda?"

Mom checked the small coin purse she kept in her larger purse. If she had 10 or 15 cents, she would unfailingly give it to me. She knew that 10 cents would buy a small soda and large sodas were five cents more.

I loved going to the drugstore to people watch. As far as I know there was no place like it in the world. It acted as a strong magnet bringing in a unique cross-section in every community throughout the nation. Older retired men, people waiting for their prescriptions to be filled, teenagers and an occasional youngster sat silently or visited while sipping sodas, floats, or milkshakes. I felt special and I watched and listened attentively. Being seven only heightened my interest.

"What can I get you today?'

This was when the fun began. Usually, a young woman dressed much like a nurse, right up to the starched Nehru hat, smiled and waited for my order. I think they thought it was cute to see a seven-year-old sitting on a stool all by himself. The selections were incredible: lemon, cherry, and chocolate cokes, root beer, or even a flavored Seven-Up. If you were lucky enough to have twenty cents, tasty phosphate drinks were also available. Ice cream floats and milk shakes were usually out of the question for me because they cost too much.

"Lemon coke." I always blurted out my favorite. As I turned my head, there was usually an adult or two who smiled at the little man ordering his favorite drink. Thinking back on it, I was probably a little cheeky for my age, hopefully in an endearing rather than impertinent way.

"Sounds like a treat you really like," a waitress once said to me with a big smile.

"Yep," I replied proudly.

I started third grade at a new elementary school on the west side of town. Dixon was growing and now had almost 4,000 people. Another elementary school was needed because new homes were being quickly built on the west side of town moving in the direction of Highway 40, now I-80. My dad was appointed the first principal of West Dixon Elementary School and I transferred there. I trekked to Gruesendorf's Fountain at the Drug Store fewer and fewer times. Then the counter was taken out. A new Frosty Freeze was built downtown and an A&W Root Beer drive-in with carhop service was constructed near the freeway. Crowds packed in cars gathered at these new locations. The era of the soda fountain ended as did special trips to order my treat. Lemon cokes and phosphates went the way of the sarsaparilla. The coke and root beer generation driving cars firmly and triumphantly elbowed its way into the forefront of American culture.

Chapter 4

THE UNEXPECTED GIFT

Like most of my friends, reaching the end of the school day resulted in a burst of energy. This particular day I felt added excitement as I raced for the bike racks located on the west side of the multipurpose room at the school. My dad had bought my sister and I newly reconditioned bikes after we convinced him that we were old enough and needed a bigger model. I was bursting with pride at now being able to keep up with the older boys as well as classmates, especially when riding to school.

My excitement burst like a punctured balloon when I got to the section of the bike racks where I had left my new bike. It was gone. I was soon to encounter another of life's interesting experiences and perhaps even learn a lesson or two.

My smile turned to tears as I searched the area. Where had it gone? Was someone playing a trick on me? In those days, I thought of a prankster first because theft was not very common. I raced into the school office and through the short swinging doors separating the staff from the public where parents and students entered.

I rushed into the Principal's Office. "Dad, Dad, my bike. It's gone. Someone took my bike. It's not at the racks."

The well-groomed man at the large wooden desk looked back at me with surprise. My dad wore a nice suit and tie every day he went to work. When he went outside, he wore a brown fedora, a type of hat commonly worn by many men until the mid-1960s.

"Slow down," he said calmly. "Tell me what happened." He

then got up and we went outside together and searched the school grounds.

This was one of the few times that my dad and I walked or spoke together at the school. He had a belief that it wasn't a good idea for us to do much more than nod at each other during the time I attended "his" school. I was one of 500 students. No more. No less. Our search of the school grounds proved futile. "I'll do some investigating. You go home and I'll see you there."

That night was a long and sad one. My dad said very little except that he was sorry. An ethnic German from the Midwest, he didn't spend a lot of time in conversation. The bike had been a surprise and although it was previously owned, it was in perfect condition. We didn't have a lot of money. In those days credit cards didn't exist, and we lived paycheck to paycheck like almost everyone else. My dad had somehow splurged to buy my sister and I bikes. I was thrilled to have it and at the same time, I knew that my parents sacrificed for me.

School started the next day as it always did with us reciting the Pledge of Allegiance and then a page of math. I was unhappy but resigned. Before recess, a student monitor came into the classroom and gave my teacher a note. He looked in my direction but I thought nothing of it. As the recess bell rang, my fifth-grade teacher walked my way. This set me on edge. No one in class wanted to be too near Mr. Fritch. He was a World War ll Marine veteran who told us almost every day how soft and weak we were and how hard it was while he was growing up or fighting in the big war. He was an angry man. As I winced slightly, he bent down and whispered that my dad wanted to see me in the office.

When I entered the office, I noticed two chairs. In one chair sat an older boy named Esteban Galvan. His face was tear-stained and his head bowed. I looked at my dad and then at Esteban before I too sat down. Believe it or not, I still wasn't sure why I was there. My dad then began. He spoke softly but with authority.

"We found your bike. Yesterday after school Esteban took it and rode it home. He has admitted taking it." As usual, my dad kept things short. "He knows that what he did was wrong. Their family is poor and his father died a few years back. They have very little for other things and he's never had a bike of any kind. His teacher tells me that he's a good boy who works very hard, does his class work, and is doing well in learning English."

On the one hand I was angry that someone had done that to me. It was personal. But I also felt sorry for Esteban. I had seen him on the playground playing alone most of the time. He had three sisters who also attended the school and they were nice girls. I didn't know what to think.

My dad spoke again. "I'm giving him your bike." After a pause, he continued. "Esteban you can go." As he left the office, Esteban looked a little confused and embarrassed. I must admit that I felt the same way.

For a moment I was stunned. I didn't say a word.

"Danny, you are 10 and have had a tricycle and a bike. Esteban wanted to belong with the boys who rode their bikes to school. He felt that he would never have that chance. Do you understand?"

For another moment, I looked down. I had always respected my dad. Even the school bad boys told me now and then that they didn't like being paddled, but he was fair. This decision was not out of character for him. I was still disappointed but at that moment I had never felt prouder or more grounded in my life. There was no longer any anger at losing my bike. I respected my dad more than ever. Slowly I got up to go.

"Danny?" My dad's face softened. "This weekend we'll go to Sacramento and buy you a new bike." I nodded and a smile crossed my face and lasted all the way until I reentered the classroom and saw Mr. Fritch. I was learning that life is complicated and that anger, compassion, and wisdom intersect and touch us in odd ways. How we react is up to us.

Chapter 5

THE ACCORDION BAND

Each large room with shiny linoleum floors contained 20 to 30 hospital beds holding young men in various stages of recovery or rehabilitation. Often a wheelchair was positioned in front of the beds. They all wore blue pajamas. Those sitting in wheelchairs wore thin white slippers. White plaster castes of all kinds, from small to large, were wrapped on arms and legs, some were held up by small cranes and wire connected to metal pulleys.

"My little accordion band is happy to be here to play songs for you. Everyone will tell you their name and then we'll start. I'm Danny," I announced in a serious voice while giving way to the other five members of the band. Being half-German and half-Norwegian doomed me at an early age to a painful inability to speak and smile at the same time.

Occasionally, someone in an audience whispered, "What a serious young man!" Snickers floated from those assembled. For some reason, the accordion teacher and organizer of these events had picked me to be the band's leader. I was mortified to be pushed up in front of the audience, including my dad, who always drove us to events. But I had no choice.

We had arrived early at David Grant Hospital on Travis Air Force Base to "cheer up the troops." The airmen who occupied the rooms seemed to enjoy seeing us, or maybe we broke the monotony of the hospital a little, but I felt a small twinge of satisfaction to think that we were helping them in some way.

"Our first song is 'Lady of Spain.' We hope you like it." In 1957 I was 10 and had played the accordion for almost three years, halfway through the accordion-playing part of my childhood. I had no natural talent and loathed playing. If the practice and lessons weren't bad enough, there were always invitations throughout the year to perform for various local groups like the Dixon Women's Improvement Club, the Lions Club, and talent shows of all kinds. Sometimes we were even asked to dress up in our Sunday clothes or a costume of some kind, especially around holidays.

The Dixon Women's Improvement Club, made up of strong-willed, civic-minded women, invited us often and was one of the largest clubs in town. Community old timers remarked that the club's dynamic start began in the 1880s to fight the influence of the numerous bars located on every corner and the houses of ill repute that were tucked away on side streets. Most of the women wore small, simple hats and were steely eyed and committed to the cause of decency and civic improvement. Throughout the years, they attracted like-minded adherents who worked on beautification projects year- round. In the late 50s, there I stood, playing "Lady of Spain."

The accordion experience was my dad's idea. He loved the thought of someone in the family standing and entertaining a crowd or playing for a dance. One of his childhood heroes was Lawrence Welk. My dad and Lawrence Welk grew up separately in North Dakota but were from a unique group of Germans whose ancestors lived for 200 years in Russia. The polite name today is *Germans from Russia* but there were many other names less complimentary like *Roosians* or *Krauts*. Even German immigrants known by scholars as *Reichsdeutsche* didn't claim them and stayed their distance from the rough-hewn Germans with strange accents, foods, and clothes. When Lawrence Welk hit it big with his bands playing swing music, tens of thousands of Germans from Russia in the Midwest, especially the Dakotas, rejoiced, and he became an admired figure that thousands of Midwesterners identified with. In America, that model still happens often. Down inside, my dad wished that I would become another Lawrence Welk. I wanted to play baseball.

At some point, I disappointed my dad and left the accordion, "Lady of Spain," and polka favorites like the "She's Too Fat for Me Polka." My mother, and later my wife, never let me get rid of my accordion and after 55 years it's packed away somewhere in the garage. I still scrunch up my face when someone mentions the accordion days, but my dad put a positive spin on the experience by saying I reaped the benefits of "getting in front of an audience," which he considered an important lifetime skill that was "money in the bank." He was a pretty wise Roosian.

Chapter 6

THE TOXIC DDT FOG

I wonder sometimes how we survived what we did as kids. I also wonder how my parents, and my friends' parents, weren't arrested for negligence or worse. The only explanation is that parents in the middle of the 20th century, at least in California, didn't coddle their children. They expected their kids to get up and dust themselves off, no matter how many times they fell or were knocked down. Children were expected to fight their own battles and learn from adversity. In many ways, I believe that the people who lived in California when I was a child were as ornery as a bunch of Texas wranglers who, at the end of a long day, can't find the chuck wagon. Yet the tough old West Coast culture came apart in the mid-1960s with the Summer of Love, the Age of Aquarius and acid rock. Until this occurred, we were engaging in behavior unimaginable today. Coddling was not a virtue, but we didn't know the difference.

"Here it comes," yelled Alex Yandel, one of my friends from West F Street.

"Yeah, I see it," said Darryl Kleeberger, my best friend until we graduated from Dixon High in 1966. "What a fog! The street lights are covered and you can't see anything in the flat tops."

The "flat tops" was a housing project that had been built soon after WWII to house GIs coming back from the war. They were made of concrete and had flat top roofs that had long since gone out of style. I had a friend or two who lived in the "flat tops but I knew it was best to stay on our side of North Washington Street, which served as the line between neighborhoods.

We gathered as a group of about ten kids. By today's standards, that's a lot, but I can't remember a house that didn't have at least one child and most had at least two. The Hulls had six kids, but they were needed to deliver milk every morning for the family dairy business. Our group ranged in age from 9 to 12. Everyone chirped with excited conversation while waiting as the fog rolled our way. No one had been called to dinner yet, and those who had had convinced their parents to allow them a few more minutes to stay outside and enjoy the fun.

"Time to come home for dinner, Danny," my sister yelled from our front yard.

"Tell Mom that I'll be in after we ride with the fog machine," I responded. I stayed and no one else went home as night and darkness enveloped the streets.

The fog drifted closer as a large model pick-up truck pulled a four-wheeled trailer steadily down the street. The trailer carried a dirty white tank with a sprayer that threw out a huge cloud of a mosquito-killing DDT solution. The streets of Dixon were sprayed twice a year, once at the start of summer and once at the end of the summer.

We didn't just watch the truck and tank drive past. No, that wouldn't have been any fun. "Are you ready?" I yelled as I scanned my friends sitting on their bicycles. "Follow me. Let's go."

We all took off after the tank trailer and got as close as we could to the spray apparatus while the toxic solution spewed into the air. Larry Bailey and Darryl liked to grab a hold of the side of the tank rig so they could be pulled up the street while the rest of us rode through the heavy mist and attempted to avoid crashing into unseen bike riders cruising a few feet away. We knew the possibility of hitting the back of the trailer and getting knocked to the street existed. We thought in terms of skill level rather than the danger we were facing.

Most of us pulled out of the cloud when the truck made the turn at the end of F Street onto Adams Street and went home for dinner. Sometimes we would decide to take the long route home and ride until we got tired before turning around and heading back. Finally, someone must have read the book *Silent Spring* by Rachel Carson because the accepted mosquito abatement practices came to a merciful end, but for us, ignorance was bliss.

"Wash up for dinner, Danny," my mom always reminded me when I got home. "Be sure to fold your play clothes so you can use them to finish out the week. I'm busy washing your school clothes."

As far as I know, except for Darryl, who died in a freak accident a month after graduation, members of the West F group are still alive. Somehow, we survived the fog and the adversity and ignorance of those years.

Chapter 7

THE NUT PICKERS OF DIXON

"How many full bags do we have now?" I asked for at least the third time in an hour.

"Three regular gunny sacks and one large one filled to the top. We're going to make a lot of money today," said Alex Yandel, who lived across the street from me on West F with his parents and two brothers and two sisters. Alex was two years younger than me and the same age as my sister, Dian. He was an ordinary kid of average height and weight for his age, a distinguishing feature caused many people to stare and occasionally ask questions. His chest, right shoulder, and the lower part of his neck carried the scars of a terrible accident that had occurred when he was two years old. He had pulled a pan of boiling water off the stove and the water flowed down his chest melting the flesh into a rough texture like the moon's surface. Alex never mentioned it though or whether the scar bothered him in any way.

We raced home after school to change our clothes before pushing my old red wagon out of the garage. We needed to get out to the country road near our subdivision before other kids our age arrived. A brisk north wind had been blowing since the night before, creating perfect conditions for making money.

"It's getting dark. We 'd better head back to town. We won't be able to take the walnuts to the Farmers' Exchange until tomorrow," I yelled over to Alex. He had brought his wagon so we divided up the sacks for the short trip home. We easily pulled our wagons the mile to our street.

During the fall months, many kids our age picked walnuts from the ground after school and over the weekends to make extra money. We made a dollar a gunny sack for Black Walnuts and were paid by the weight for English walnuts or almonds. The Black Walnuts were easy to find because the rural roads in Solano and Yolo Counties were heavily planted with Black Walnut trees as wind breaks. Heavy winds knocked the nuts down in large numbers onto the roads and the ditches. Black walnuts weren't in big demand and weren't farmed commercially since they were so hard to extract from the shell although early in the 1930s someone invented a machine that cracked open the nut and made their collection more profitable. The nut meat was also smaller than the English varieties. We made eight to ten dollars apiece a week in season.

On the way home, Alex mused, "I sure hope Mr. Timm lets us go into his orchard tomorrow and pick nuts. We'll make a killing if he'll let us scrounge the almond orchard." Malcom Timm owned a parcel of land on the east side of Highway 40. His family had emigrated to our part of Solano County from Denmark at the end of the 1800's. He farmed one of the few orchards of English Walnuts and almonds in our area of Solano County. At the end of his harvest, he sometimes allowed kids from town to pick walnuts by hand. Sometimes he paid for the sacks himself and other times, late in the season, he allowed us to take the walnuts to the Farmers' Exchange. Thirty to thirty-five dollars a bag was standard payment for English walnuts and forty to fifty for almonds. It took a lot of time and energy to fill one sack, but we made big money.

The Farmers' Exchange was a locally owned hardware and variety store. Similar stores were located in most small communities throughout the country. Those working in hardware stores generally owned the small business unlike the big box stores of today.

"Mr. Carpenter, we have sacks of nuts," I reported to Milt Carpenter, one of the owners and the grandson of one of Dixon's oldest families. He and Bill Fairfield, who doubled as the chief of the local volunteer fire department, were always in the store unless a fire had been signaled by the citywide siren. At those times, the store was locked until the fire was brought under control. I thought that no one in the store worked very hard as men from town congregated near the counters standing or drew up chairs to gossip, drink coffee, and talk politics. I never saw anyone greet potential customers or dust shelves. Locals were greeted by a quick "Morning, Jim." On occasion, someone would bring in a bag of squirrel tails. They were paid 25 cents a tail as they were considered pests.

Alex and I split the nut money and felt really good about the money we made for the week. Sometimes we worked with a whole gang of kids who lived in the neighborhood, but splitting the money six or seven ways usually meant less money although it was more fun.

Neighborhood kids don't seem to collect nuts like we did back when fewer people lived in the area. There are fewer trees for many of the huge, old black walnuts were cut down to widen the roads. English walnut trees and almond trees are now mechanically harvested and swept by machines so few nuts are left on the ground. Innovation and machines make all the difference. Another reason kids don't work in picking up nuts is that the price of nuts is still what it was 50 years ago. Money made doesn't go far in today's economy for the time spent working. Finally, Americans don't allow their children to roam free unless heavily supervised, so immigrant groups and families with buckets pick up the few black walnuts still available on country roads.

Chapter 8

THE ONE-ROOM DAKOTA SCHOOLHOUSE

I knew the importance of detouring from our trip to Minnesota to this location inside a North Dakota wheat field in the summer of 1958. My father became quieter than usual and looked back and forth with increased scrutiny.

"What are you looking for, Dad?" I asked although I knew we were looking for a one -room schoolhouse where he had taught kindergarten to eighth grade before the start of World War ll. But everything looked the same to me and had for many miles.

Dad said nothing and kept driving slowly on the dusty dirt road. My mom, sister, and I sat back and allowed him space as he searched the fields for some familiar marker known only to him. By asking, I guess I wanted to break the monotony so common in North Dakota of mile after mile of the same view. I didn't realize that what I heard on this day would be far more interesting than what I saw. The North Dakota landscape was one of rolling hills covered by short yellow wheat stalks recently harvested by farmers driving huge modern machines. During my dad's early years on his family farm, they used large horse teams.

Suddenly, as we drove up a short incline, a small white building appeared in the distance. It seemed to float as if on a golden sea and was the only manmade object visible in any direction. My sister and I rose up in the back seat to get a better view with the anticipation of reaching our destination.

"There, Dad. There it is," my sister yelled.

My sister Dian was two years younger. Her nose and cheeks were lightly sprinkled with freckles. She favored her hair long and the color alternated from a darker auburn to a California sun-drenched blond. Unlike my skin, hers tolerated very little sun before it turned quickly to painful red. Until recently I always thought of myself as the lucky one who spent lots of time in the sun and had the annual summer tan. Now I see the dermatologist on a regular basis because of sun-damaged skin.

The white building resembled any number of small older churches or farm houses I'd seen near where we lived in California. The notable differences here included a missing steeple and cross.

My dad perked up and he sped up a bit. We all piled out of the car and happily ran around the small building. Even my dad walked with an added purpose as he looked at the small windows and simple wood construction while Dian and I ran around like the kids we were without giving attention to any particular detail. We were happy to have reached our destination. My dad tried the front door and it slowly opened. One can only guess the images stirred up as memories like dust kicked up from the floor after so many years.

My first impression was that the inside room was too small. "Could 18 to 20 students from ages 5 to 13 really sit and learn in such a place?" I thought.

Several old desks were strewn around the room. A black pot-bellied stove sat in a corner in the back of the room. On a front wall a worn-out blackboard was still in place but the black had deteriorated to a faded gray. To be honest, I was somewhat disappointed by the simple shabbiness everywhere I looked.

Dad walked over to the stove and shook his head. My sister and I followed closely behind. "What's that for?" she asked.

"It's used to heat the room," he said wistfully. We had always lived in houses with central air and heating although some homes were equipped with wood-burning stoves as a fashion statement. "I had to bring lumps of coal to school in the morning and start the stove fire before the students arrived during the long winter months." He suddenly smiled as a small laugh escaped. Stories of his time as the school's teacher started to flow as if a lid had been twisted off a jar.

He told us he lived for a month at a time with families that had children attending the school as part of his pay. They gave him a bed and cooked him breakfast and dinner before sending him to work with a lunch. The salary for a teacher in a rural district was pitifully small. "I had to carry my books, lunch, coal and a small bucket of water for as far as five miles to school," he explained. Sometimes he decided not to pack coal or water depending on the weather conditions. If he got thirsty, he might sneak to where students stored their water buckets and take a drink of their water during recess. "On one occasion, after recess, I heard a tussle in the back of the room and saw two boys scuffling. After separating the boys, I learned that one boy had been accused of stealing water from someone else's bucket. After that, I started bringing my own water again, but it was hard and I had to stop and rest more often on my way to school."

Dad had no car and he walked most of the time in good weather or bad. If he was lucky, the parents at the home where he was staying had horses and occasionally, he was allowed to ride one to school. This worked out well until he was kicked in the head by a horse and decided that he wasn't cut out for teaching in North Dakota. He and a couple of friends chipped in to buy a car and drove to California in 1940. Soon thereafter, the war started and he joined the Navy.

As we drove back to the main road on the way to Minnesota to meet Grandma Johnson, my dad said for everyone to hear, "Man, I'm sure glad I made it to California."

Chapter 9

THE VISIT TO MEET GRANDMA JOHNSON

"How would you like to go to Minnesota to meet Grandma Johnson?" my mother asked one day in the spring of 1958. "You'll meet your uncles, aunts, and cousins and see the farm." My grandfather and my grandmother had split up after two years of marriage and he moved to Canada. No one ever mentioned him and I never met him or even saw his photo.

"Farm?" My interest perked up. "Do they have animals and tractors?"

"They sure do," my mother replied, "but we are going so that you and your sister can meet your grandmother. She wants to meet you two."

"I guess so." I replied.

I don't want to seem indifferent about meeting my grandmother but it had never crossed my mind that we would be able to meet since it meant traveling all the way in our car to visit with relatives in the Midwest. Airplanes were expensive and out of the question. It was so far away that no one from Minnesota had visited us, and we had never driven further than Reno to visit one of my mother's sisters, Aunt Gladys.

Besides, no one I knew had contact with their grandparents. In our neighborhood, almost everyone was from somewhere else. The Baileys and Basingers were from Appalachia and their families came to California to work in the meat processing houses in Dixon. The Yandels landed in Dixon after their dad retired from the Air Force out of Travis Air Force Base. The Kleebergers were from Canada and the Hulls moved from Illinois to run a dairy. Almost every other family

I knew moved to California after the war. Their grandparents lived elsewhere. My dad's mother died before I was born. Grandparents didn't exist in my small world.

"We're going to have a great time on the way and a better time when we get there," Mom said as we left for our long drive east.

There were significant ups and downs on the trip.

"Mom, could you please stop smoking?" Every hour in the car, my sister and I traded turns begging my mother to stop smoking. In those days, she was a chain smoker who thought nothing of smoking in the car and was oblivious to the effects of smoke that rolled slowly but continuously into the back half of the car as defiantly as a fog bank rolling into San Francisco in July. Cars in those days didn't have air conditioning and we suffered hour after hour. The drive through Nevada in mid-summer was torture.

Things got worse in Utah. "I can't stand it!" I yelled. My sister screamed and cried. We stopped at the Great Salt Lake in Utah to swim. When we finished there were signs at public outdoor showers for all bathers to rinse off. My sister and I only wanted to get towel dried, get back on the road, and leave the desert. About an hour later, in 100 degree heat, our bodies salted over with a crust from head to toe. Next to getting a tooth drilled for a filling, this was the worst sensation I'd ever encountered. Eventually my dad stopped at a gas station and hosed us off.

As we traveled day after day, I started thinking about Grandma Johnson. Who would she turn out to be? Why didn't I know much about her? Was she a stern and unpleasant lady? We knew she was strong-willed. She'd grown up in Norway and emigrated alone when she was a teenager. Her life on the farm in Norway was hard. At an early age she was up by four to milk cows. In the spring, she, her sisters and cousins, drove the cows into mountain valleys and stayed there to milk the cows and make cheese for months on end until they walked home in late summer. Raising five children on a dairy in Minnesota was also difficult. Would I pass muster? Even my mother, who was sometimes stern, spoke of Grandma Johnson with a kind of reverence. "What if she doesn't like me," I kept thinking.

"We're here." my mother announced. Instinctively my sister, ducked down so that only the top part of her head was visible in the back seat. We scanned our surroundings. A large barn squatted in the background. It wasn't like a California barn as the roof swept down and curved out like a Dutch bonnet. Fences seemed to go in every direction and we saw several pens on either side of the barn with brown milk cows unlike the black-and-white Holsteins near Dixon. In the distance were large hogs with huge, ugly heads peering at us through the fence in the furthest pen.

"Hello, hello." A tall lady with wide strong shoulders walked quickly our way. Her silver hair was rolled up in a bun. She wore a long straight dress that dropped down just short of her ankles. On it was a white apron. On her feet were black work shoes. I could see that she was smiling, which was a good sign. We all hugged and I noticed that she had the biggest hands I had ever seen. We met my Uncles Harold and Norval and Aunts Margaret and Ruth, and then we entered the large white farmhouse. I thought my mother was tall at five feet nine inches, but Grandma Johnson stood closer to five foot, ten inches. She was taller than my mother and my father.

In due time I met cousins Randall, Raynard, and Rosalie. Randall was 4 and constantly saying, "Ja sure." For three days, we ate, played, and got to know each other. Five meals a day were served: coffee and pastry at 5 am, breakfast at 8, dinner at 1, lunch at 4, and supper at 7. Grandma Johnson made everything from scratch. We giggled at the number of times we ate each day while on the farm. One afternoon before dinner grandma played the old pump organ and sang.

She said, "Oh, Ja" a lot. She left Norway forty years before, but she still had the Scandinavian accent I came to associate with people from that part of the world. She also smiled and laughed more often than anyone else.

I spent much of my time running around the farm playing on mountains of harvested corn and scrambling up farm equipment of all types. No one seemed to be particularly alarmed by our play or our explorations of the property. The only warning I received was from Uncle Norval. "Don't ever go into the hog pen. They're dangerous."

In a short time, I became close with my Minnesota family. Grandma turned out to be a sweet, happy lady who was genuinely pleased that we came to meet her. Dian and I played with our cousins up to the time we left.

"Hey, Randall. You wanna get some corn and go down and feed the hogs?"

"Ja sure."

I only wished I had Grandma Johnson in my life more often. I realized that I missed out on something special living so far away. Kids need grandparents.

Chapter 10

THE LOCAL BUTLER

Growing up in Dixon during the mid-20th century provided few experiences that might be considered out of the ordinary. Life rolled on in a routine manner most of the time. Even when Herb Caen, the iconic and fabled gossip columnist for the *San Francisco Chronicle* described Dixon in the 1950s as "having more millionaires per capita" than any city in California, most folks smiled and shook their heads. If there really was that kind of money in town, it belonged to those old pioneer families who were considered "land rich" rather than California's *nuevo- rich* with large bank accounts. These families were, even then, considered dinosaurs and were mostly long gone. Then again, maybe Herb Caen knew what he was talking about.

"Master Dale, may I serve you a before-dinner drink this evening?" The smooth-as -silk voice belonged to a large black man named George wearing a formal butler's uniform with a short white jacket, shirt, and black tie. His pants were smartly creased and touched shiny black patent leather shoes.

"I'll have an orange juice, George." answered Dale Taylor, my best friend from third grade. Dale was slightly larger than me, and he was always perfectly groomed in expensive play clothes bought at upscale stores in Sacramento or the Bay Area. Most of the other kids I knew wore jeans and a t-shirt. Not Dale, whose appearance was always impeccable no matter what the occasion.

"And you, Master Daniel? What may I get you this evening?" I wanted to say, *a large coke* but decided I should follow Dale's lead and ask for a glass of orange juice. I looked up at George as he nodded slightly and turned to walk back to the Taylors' two-story white house, which had been built sometime in the late 19th century. Many similar homes were sprinkled on farm land in rural Solano and Yolo Counties and they belonged to successful farm families. The old Peterson Estate, where the Taylors lived was two miles south of Dixon. Mrs. Taylor, a Peterson descendent, usually drove her four-door black Cadillac with red leather seats into town to pick me up on Saturday morning. Dale and I would sit in the back and I felt oddly special, like royalty. I would stay overnight and go home on Sunday.

As I watched George walk slowly back to the house, I noticed that his posture and gait were perfect and his short white hair added to the formal setting I wasn't used to.

"Hey, let's play catch before dinner," I suggested. Dale and I shared a love of baseball and although I played in Dixon's youth league, Dale wanted only to play catch and practice his hitting. We not only played catch but moved on to the old baseball favorites of "flies up" to practice catching outfield flies and "hot pepper" to sharpen our fielding skills.

George brought us the juice on a silver tray. He left us as we took a short break. At the sound of the dinner bell, a giant iron triangle being slapped by a foot-long metal bar, we headed into the house. George held out a chair and seated us one at a time. Dale's mom said a prayer and then George and his wife Minnie, who was the cook, served us. I assume she also cleaned the house during the day but I have no recollection of her daytime duties as we spent most of our time outside playing baseball, swimming in the pool, or exploring the barns.

The Taylors wanted Dale to attend the best West Coast prep school and found a fit with the Robert Lewis Stevenson Academy in Pebble Beach, California. Before the start of 4th grade, the Taylors moved to the Del Monte Forest on the golf course and I never saw Minnie or George again.

While I was best man at his wedding after he graduated from Stanford University, I lost track of Dale over the years. Recently, using the Internet, I located his cousin who reported that Dale had died an alcoholic a few years back. As I think back on my experiences with the Taylors, I'm left with equal parts sadness and amazement at how life unfolds in ways we don't expect. This information about Dale left me confused and full of questions. I wondered what had happened to him. I also wondered what had happened to George and Minnie. When and where did their work life begin? Did they find employment after they left the Taylors? Were other families seeking domestic help to match their unique skills? I was an observer with a peek back at an era that had mostly ended in America before the start of the 20th century when service from a formal butler was more common. Unique events occur as life rolls by. Sometimes we need to slow down, take notice, and recognize their existence.

Chapter 11

THE DANCE CARD

I was nervous and excited in equal parts sitting in the old multipurpose room at my first school dance. Then I saw Diana Green walking from the girls' side of the room toward us. Sitting with my 7th grade friends, we tried hard to act like we'd been there before. We hadn't. A variety of behaviors erupted and most were immature to downright silly. I sat on a fold-up chair afraid to move a muscle.

"Hi, Danny, I need someone to sign my dance card for the ninth dance. Would you sign my card?" Diana said in a soft voice. As far as I knew, this was the only way Diana spoke. Her voice was always soft, sweet and pleasant to the ear.

"Me?" The only muscle moving was in my lips. I froze and thought I was the victim of a hoax or a joke of some kind. Then I remembered that Diana Green's reputation in the school as an eighth grader was perfect. Everyone I knew liked her and admired her kindness. She was nice to everyone including seventh graders like me at a time when many junior high schoolers were self-centered, critical, and insecure. The pecking order for junior high school rivals only that of large chicken coops.

I saw that my friends had either opened their eyes and mouths as wide as possible, or they were looking back and forth at one another like they had a glimpse of their first *Playboy Magazine.*

"Okay." Oh, no. I couldn't believe my response was so lame. *Okay?* That was the dumbest response ever, and I have regretted uttering it for almost sixty years. Dance cards were handed out at the beginning of the dance and were required of all students attending. I signed and Diana signed mine before turning and walking back to the eighth-grade side where most of the girls were sitting.

Eighth grade boys like Bert Caldwell and Richard Machado, the most popular boys in school, easily circulated throughout the room talking and laughing with boys and girls from the seventh and eighth grade attending the first sock hop of the year. My friends and I sat and watched. It was called a sock hop because everyone in the dance checked their shoes at the door. A few couples sat next to each other, mostly on the eighth-grade side. Socially inept seventh grade boys played games of tag from time to time completely unaware of dance expectations and social etiquette. Others nervously tried to figure out what came next.

Most of my friends were showing various stages of agitation and disbelief. Many spent the rest of the dance rolling their eyes. I didn't know either, and my anxiety leapt to a new level. My friends punched my arm and I was the butt of jokes and silly remarks. Several student body officers, including the social director, an elected position, stood at the front of the room on a small stage playing records and announcing the number of the dance and the type of dance to be played next. A small number of girls brought records and pleaded with the social director to play their record or make a dedication to a special boy. There were *snowballs* where the record was stopped to allow couples who were dancing the time to find a new partner. This encouraged reluctant or shy students to be pulled out onto the dance floor. *Lady's choice* dances let girls ask boys to dance. The number of dancers on the floor increased then since girls always seemed more willing to dance than boys, especially when it came to the seventh-grade crowd. Most of my friends were wrestled out to the floor for these dances at least once, but I sat waiting for the ninth dance.

I don't remember the ninth dance being called, but it was a slow dance. I remember staying an arm's length away as we shuffled our feet on the floor. Diana smiled the whole time. Her dark blond hair was short and immaculately styled. She had the most beautiful, blue eyes I had ever seen with a perfect complexion and full creamy lips. I tried to smile but my mouth was too dry. I felt like I had returned from the Mojave Desert minutes before.

"Thank you, Danny. That wasn't so bad, was it?"

I almost fainted. "No. Not really." I stammered and tried to smile.

I walked back to my chair ignoring the taunts and questions from my friends as we waited out the end of the dance. I was in some kind of bubble and slowly floated home. What Diana did was simply a *random act of kindness*. I know I'll never forget it.

Chapter 12

THE ACCIDENT

My parents were comfortable in a small-town environment. They understood that growing up in heartland America in the mid-20th century included unwritten but strong rituals for young boys and girls coming of age. One tradition was connecting boys to guns and hunting.

"Dad, I saw a gun on sale at the Farmers' Exchange. Mr. Fairfield told me that he only had one left. Can we go down and take a look?" I began to make plans to plead my case since my dad's experience with guns wasn't a positive one, but he understood the attraction.

Yet my dad tried to talk me out of getting a gun. When he was young, his dad had bought him a rifle, but he didn't like killing animals for sport. I should have listened to him. Still, I pleaded my case and dragged him to Farmers Exchange where we bought a single shot 20-gauge Remington.

"A single shot is good enough and you must be trained properly in its use," Dad said sternly.

"Okay," I almost shouted. "I will be the most careful hunter you ever saw." At 14, I took a Hunter Safety course taught by local members of the National Rifle Association, and I was ready to be a hunter.

On a November day in 1962, Tom Sork, a high school friend, invited a group of us to hunt on his farm. His family owned land south of Dixon. "I've been seeing a lot of pheasants in those fields and my dad says there are a lot of birds this year."

Meeting Tom were Darryl Kleeberger, Bill Wentworth, Hal Hanna, and I. The five of us walked the cut milo corn fields, which provided nice cover and ample food for pheasants. Bill released his excited gray Weimaraner. We immediately set out walking the harvested fields of corn stalks leaning into a strong north wind. The dog immediately jumped a small group of pheasants. The task at this point was to raise our guns and identify within seconds which birds were female and which were the more colorful males and our targets.

The birds gained height and started frantically flapping their wings. Due to the direction of the wind, the birds flew or were blown back in our direction. As we tracked the birds, it became apparent that their path towards us made shooting unsafe as our gun barrels swung back in our direction.

"Boom."

What happened?

I was stunned. Everyone froze.

"What happened?" someone yelled.

I quickly scanned our hunting line and determined that everyone was accounted for. I couldn't tell if the noise had occurred 5 seconds or 50 seconds before. No one said anything until Darryl yelled, "Tom, what happened?'

Tom was standing but his head was tilted down toward the ground. I looked closer. Lines of red started to appear near his ears and the back of his neck.

I moved quickly to join Darryl. "Tom, are you okay? Quick, let's move him to the road." We guided Tom as the red lines expanded, became larger, a darker red and moved below his collar. The blond hair on the back of his head turned a light red, then darker by the second, especially when it reached his neck. "You stay here with Tom," I said. "I'm going for help." Everything was a blur. Seconds, minutes… I didn't know.

I ran what seemed like two miles to the Sork home. Although I was a football player and in reasonably good shape, I was out of breath after my first few steps. My legs were heavy. Why couldn't I run?

As I reached the large ranch house, I opened the back door to the kitchen and found his parents sitting at a breakfast nook drinking coffee. At first, they smiled. That changed quickly to worry.

"What do I say?" I thought. "Someone's been shot" was all I could offer.

"Who, who was it?" they seemed to shout in unison.

"Tom," I said weakly.

Mr. Sork jumped up and ran out the door. I followed. He ran to his truck as I yelled. "We're on the north fields".

He revved up the engine and I jumped in the truck bed, a move I instantly regretted. The truck swung wildly with each turn as I tried to hold on to anything I could to stay in one place and not be pounded back and forth between the bed walls. Then we arrived. The truck slid to a stop.

Everyone was exactly as I l had left them and I remember thinking, "How strange." Darryl held Tom, who was still sitting up on the dirt road. Hal and Bill were in the field looking at their guns.

Somehow Mr. Sork loaded Tom into the truck and headed back toward the ranch where they called an ambulance. The next thing I remember I was standing with Darryl looking at the guys in the field still frozen and seemingly still in shock. Suddenly Bill started unchambering his shells. "I've got all of my shells," he yelled.

"I've got mine," everybody else repeated one after another. Someone even suggested that we finish our day hunting. Darryl and I stared in disbelief. Hal later admitted to firing the shot. He endured occasional teasing, but he was well liked at school and his mistake was soon forgotten.

Tom survived after a horrifying trip to the hospital where the police car taking him to an ambulance got into an accident at an intersection in Dixon. He had been shot squarely in the back of his head. After three months, some of it spent in the hospital, Tom returned to school. To this day, he still has scars on both sides of his head where pellets opened his skin to the bone, and about 15 pellets reside somewhere in his skull. Tom now works in the Department of Agriculture at the University of British Columbia and is in great shape and healthy in every respect. Many attending thought he was the youngest-looking member of the class at our 50th reunion in the summer of 2016.

I stopped hunting in 1962 after the accident. I can only imagine what my dad was thinking after this event. Outside of asking how I was, he never said a word.

Chapter 13

THE MEXICO TRIP: PART 1

In March 1963, my dad received a phone call from his cousin, Irene, who lived in Lodi, California. I think Irene was my dad's favorite cousin. They grew up in North Dakota speaking German, both became teachers in one-room schools, and moved to California around WW ll.

Their childhood communities were tight knit and clannish. The land was homesteaded by ethnic German farmers who emigrated from Russia between 1870 and 1920. They were talented farmers who were rumored to have brought the first successful wheat variety, Russian Red wheat, with them from the old country. It grew well on the Dakota plains. In Russia, they had fought fiercely to maintain their German customs, language, and traditions while resisting assimilation into Russian life. This stubborn insistence on remaining German lasted about one generation in America.

My grandparents and many uncles, aunts, and cousins had moved to Lodi. In fact, in the 1930s and 1940s, Lodi became a magnet for Dakota Germans who were tired of the life in the cold northern Midwest.

Irene's son, Steve, was my age and we saw each other often. We played and hung out together when my parents went to Lodi to visit relatives Steve and I had many interests in common and we loved sports. We played every game we could think of with his neighborhood friends. Steve received an offer to play basketball at Stanford but was more interested in his studies than athletics.

Lodi was much bigger than Dixon and there were many activities and events available to adults and children that didn't exist in our town. Steve and Aunt Irene were outstanding bowlers and bowling teams, if you were lucky enough to live in a community that had a bowling alley, was a popular activity for families then. They let me tag along sometimes and I embarrassed myself by throwing many gutter balls. Leisure activities in Dixon consisted almost entirely of the local movie theater or playing baseball on the elementary school fields. I grumbled about that often. I begged my parents to move to Lodi where life was more exciting.

One day, Aunt Irene called to encourage my dad to come to a meeting in Lodi. Interested parents of high school sophomores and juniors were invited to a presentation about the annual trip of students from Lodi High to Mexico for the summer.

"It's a regular trip and a great educational opportunity, Emer," she explained. "The trip is chaperoned by Mr. Simas and other school employees." Mr. Simas taught Spanish at Lodi High and he organized and escorted the 35 students every summer. "They need five more students and I thought Danny and a few friends in Dixon might like to go. It's really not that expensive because the trip is on buses."

After several phone calls, a meeting with Mr. Simas and parents from Dixon was arranged. I was ecstatic when the five families of some of my best friends agreed to send their children on a five-week tour south of the border. We were expected to work on our Spanish language skills and become acquainted with a Latin American culture. "I'll be able to bring up that Spanish grade," I told my dad, just in case he wavered at the last minute. I used my most serious face and was playing on the fact that he had attended a summer session in Guadalajara while working on his Master's program. Using the "learning card" worked more often than not when I really wanted something.

We all met on a Saturday morning at Lodi High and boarded a school bus. We were as excited as if the vehicle were a luxurious bullet train heading for Paris. The Dixon guys all scrambled on to claim the bench seat at the far back of the bus. From that location, we sensed safety and felt protected against the much larger group of students unknown to us.

After changing our bus for a newer, sleeker Mexican commercial one at the border, we headed for our first Mexican destination, Guaymas, in the State of Sonora. As we cruised down the two-lane Mexican highway, we saw the extremely difficult conditions in which so many people lived, especially in the arid parts of the country. Tiny tarpaper shacks with tin roofs and small three-sided stores selling American soda and Mexican beer popped up along the road. They always appeared unexpectedly and seemingly without purpose like large igneous rocks in Northern California volcano country. Most of the time we didn't say much but just stared and wondered how someone could live and raise a family in such conditions. Locals seemed friendly for they smiled and waved often. I never understood why they were so happy with smiles as constant as the desert sun. Located on the Gulf of Mexico, Guaymas is a small seaside town. The ocean was calm and looked like the placid large American lakes I visited growing up. At our hotel, we were assigned rooms, then quickly unpacked and changed into our bathing suits. Mine was a new wildly colored surf style that was long and baggy. (They really stood out when I went to Europe a few years later as quite a contrast to what the European men were wearing.)

We ran wildly with arms waving into the warm salt water of the gulf. I was in the middle of the pack and had just reached knee level when I noticed that the first group of students to hit the water had turned and were frantically heading the opposite direction toward me and out of the water. Smiles had turned to panicked screams. No one had bothered to advise us that large groups of nasty, aggressive jelly fish lived in the nearby lagoon. Obviously, these creatures did not want to share their space with young American tourists.

Long stinging tails wrapped around legs, arms, and heads in mere seconds. They were small and probably not man'o war varieties but the injuries were painful, nonetheless. Chaperones and employees of the resort hotel quickly applied vinegar and ice. Ugly red welts showed the direction and position of each swing and wrap of the fearsome tails. Jimmy Rehrmann, one of my Dixon friends, reported with a large grin that, "One Mexican guy told me to pee into a cup and pour it on the welts and that helps", but for us, this suggestion went nowhere. We learned our first valuable lesson. When visiting a different location, take some time to become acquainted with the environment to sort out potential hazards before charging in.

Chapter 14

MEXICO: PART 2

Our trip meandered through Mexico and took us to cities and mid-sized towns whose names I no longer remember. I recall that I liked the small well-to-do farming community of Los Mochis, which sadly today is a drug cartel battleground. The town's park was large and nicely shaded. It provided a canopy over the sidewalks, grass areas, picnic tables and benches, which were all well maintained. Kids and older residents, together as families, met here to enjoy the public spaces. Los Mochis helped me understand that there were parts of Mexico that didn't fit my preconceived notions of populations dragged down by poverty and I thought I might like to return someday although I never did.

We pressed on to Guadalajara, which impressed as a grand and elegant city with many parks, clean streets, open spaces, and outdoor cafés. Although an older city, it had the feel of a comparable energetic, thriving American city of the day. The citizens were nicely dressed in more casual working style clothes like the *guayaberas* shirt in white and pastel colors. Many men were wearing guayaberas shirts with the distinctive *alforzat* pleats that are commonly worn in Mexico and the Caribbean for both formal and informal occasions.

Near Guadalajara sits a large jewel of a lake called Lake Chapala. One afternoon we drove there to have lunch. As we made our way into a cozy waterfront restaurant, John Hartnet, a new Lodi friend, tapped me and with a strange look on his face and motioned me to follow him.

What kind of music is that?" he asked quietly.

At this point, we had experienced continuous typical Mexican folk music for weeks that seemed to float over every location where people gathered to socialize. As I cocked my head to listen, John blurted out, "Someone's singing 'I'll Do It My Way'. Let's go."

The popular Frank Sinatra tune floated from the lake front. As we walked timidly onto the deck jutting over the lake, we were surprised to see an American flag and a large sign on the next building identifying it as an American Legion Post. We immediately saw 50 or 60 middle-aged men and women. Sprinkled in the mix were a few older individuals with walking canes. Many wore Bermuda shorts and Hawaiian shirts. All were holding a mixed drink or a beer. Some held cigarettes as they sang. They were clearly having a great time. When they saw us, their faces lit up with recognition and there were enthusiastic waves. They took us for Americans immediately because of our blond hair and American-style clothing. For the rest of the afternoon our group was serenaded with easy-to-sing American songs and even a few military hymns. We were given sodas, vanilla ice cream, and potato chips from our patriotic new best friends. For that short time, we became the children and grandchildren these expats had left behind. I've often wondered if that American Legion Post is still active today and full of a new generation of happy warriors.

We spent three days in Mexico City. At the time it was the biggest and most impressive city I had ever visited. It's still one of the largest cities in the world. Bold stone buildings and churches, many hundreds of years old, held their locations comfortably next to tall modern office and apartment buildings. Nicely attired locals in work suits and dresses scurried by like ants heading to their next sugary meal. One of my most vivid impressions of this cosmopolitan city was the lush vegetation lining the streets and street medians and the parks. Unusual trees, fronds, and bright bougainvillea shrubs softened the effect of concrete and stone. Open space was lush emerald green sprinkled with colorful tropical flowers.

At one point we stopped to watch men and women performing a religious act of devotion by walking on their knees in the direction of an old cathedral for what seemed like the length of a football field.

Most held rosaries and muttered soft prayers as they made their way slowly into the ancient church. Members of our group laughed or scoffed at this expression of devotion. Overall, however, their faith impressed even the most secular among the group.

Election season transformed the street scenes with colorful swaths including banners, flags, and huge portraits painted onto every available space. As we drove through the city, we could see that the most popular politician belonged to the RRI party as their colors and letters overshadowed a political party known as PAN as well as other minor political parties by a 5 to 1 margin. The well-groomed workers walking quickly toward their places of business smiled and waved at the bus load of young friendly faces.

Other excursions into the country found us deep inside caves, riding boats on ancient Aztec canals, and climbing huge, smooth rock pyramids so tall that after climbing to the top, we could literally see for dozens of miles in all directions. We viewed huge stone slabs used for human sacrifices. At the time, there was freedom to explore these areas in ways not available today. We climbed around and up the pyramid at will as if it were on any school playground for student use at recess. Today, guides take up groups in tightly controlled formations walking only on the main steps, if they're lucky enough to do that.

Another time on the Pacific Coast, paying a dollar was a small amount to watch cliff divers lay out like birds and fall into the rolling Pacific waters off the coastal cliffs of Acapulco. This was one of the first coastal cities in Mexico that was developed with western style high rise hotels, dance clubs, and expensive jewelry stores.

Mazatlan, on the western shore of the State of Sinaloa, forever captured my imagination. I've been back at least seven times since 1963. Beautiful white beaches, tropical trees and vegetation parallel the small two-lane road hugging the Pacific Ocean north and south as far as the eye can see. In those early days, settled into the long ribbon of beaches were palm frond cabanas covering tables and chairs where people drank 10 cent beer or soda and ate fresh cooked shrimp from wooden bowls for 30 cents each. Those days are gone and Mazatlan has many cheap looking hotels and commercial buildings of all kinds but the memories of a simpler place remain strong.

Mexico turned out to be much more interesting than I had expected, with an exciting history, beautiful attractions, and friendly people. There was still unbelievable poverty and the Mexican people struggled with trash collection, sewer infrastructure, clean water, and providing enough food to feed families. However, for us, what started out as an educational experience, turned into something more profound and personal. After a half century, these memories remain strong and vivid to this day. Mr. Simas, the director and trip leader, loved Mexico: the place and its people. With his guidance and commitment, the trip evolved into a first rate set of adventures and unbelievable experiences.

Chapter 15

THE BARNYARD FIGHT

I tripped and fell as I scrambled away from the group following me. Since the rounded wall was hard to hide behind safely, I had to get up and push forward without delay. A sense of panic came in waves as adrenalin pumped through my fourteen-year old body. I was determined not to be caught by those chasing me. I couldn't tell if they were getting closer or whether my long strides had provided a safe distance to continue my retreat, and then I saw them out of the corner of my eye.

"No. I give!" I yelled as I got to my feet. I hoped they might pause for a second or two, but that strategy rarely worked. Something whizzed by my head and I heard sounds in front of me in my path of escape. I had to push on. I crouched, ran, and maneuvered in a zigzag. If I made it to the barn, I might still get away.

Outside the corn silo was the worst place to get caught. There was no place to hide or take cover. I veered right and ran as fast as I had ever run in my life. I knew what had happened to Allan when he was caught earlier in an unexpected ambush. The rotten eggs had coated his head and run down the side of his face. His blond hair was covered with an ugly slimy orange mess as sections of his hair darkened and lumped together. The worst part? When he started getting the dry heaves and wretched uncontrollably, overcome by a putrid smell hard to describe to those unaccustomed to barnyards. No matter how hard we tried to fight it off, the urge to heave overcame all other bodily functions except breathing. We'd spent the morning collecting as many bad, rotten eggs as we could find before splitting up.

"Run! Run! I'll cover you! We're in here." It was Ricky Sequeira, one of my best friends. His father owned the dairy where we held our egg fight that we'd planned earlier in the week at school. Projectiles started flying in the opposite direction over my head towards where I had tripped a few seconds earlier and hit those chasing me.

"Ha, ha, ha, ha" was all I heard as I passed Ricky and Darryl. "I got him right in the head!" Ricky screamed with a demented laugh. Ricky was small for his age but scrappy with a socially inappropriate sense of humor. He had the dark hair and thick eyebrows of his dad, who was an offspring of Portuguese immigrants who settled in the Sacramento and San Joaquin Valleys in the early part of the 20th century to farm and operate dairies. His mom had donated the blue eye color and despite his small size, all the girls thought he was cute.

Darryl Kleeberger yelled from the side of the large barn door, "They've stopped. Let's get'em."

He and Ricky charged forward with hands full of eggs. After chasing and throwing at me, our enemies were low on "ammunition" and turned back. I quickly reloaded at a conveniently placed pile of eggs on a hay bale and joined the fray. Since Allan hadn't rejoined the action, the three of us ran screaming out of the barn, and it was our turn to do the chasing.

Rick Carter, David Nishikawa, Doug Haight, and Keith Cameron turned and traced a path around the side of the silo and headed in the opposite direction toward the haystack where they had built a fort out of hay bales. Once there, we stopped and were forced to turn around and run back to the safety of our hay barn fort. In a week, the outside alfalfa bales would be moved in and prepared for winter feed for the Holsteins. Ricky's dad was not keen on us playing our games once the hay was inside for the winter.

"Wait up," Allan yelled as he jogged in our direction. "I thought I would never stop throwing up." His hair was still damp and sticky-looking, but he'd found an outdoor faucet used to fill buckets to water the cows and washed off as much of the putrid orange egg yolk as possible. "I'm not sure I want to do this anymore. I'm not coming back. These wars stink."

We laughed with Allan as he held his nose.

"Yeah, sure," I answered.

"It's getting late," replied Darryl. "I have homework to redo for school tomorrow. I'd better go."

"Okay, I'm thirsty anyway. Let's get the other guys and get some milk from the cooling tank," Ricky said. The early morning milking had been completed hours earlier and was in the refrigerated tank waiting to be picked up by the Crystal Dairy milk truck and taken to the plant in Sacramento.

We loved to finish our days getting fresh, cold milk from a spigot at the bottom of the tank that ran into large metal cups hanging nearby. For whatever reason, fresh, cold milk at the dairy is the best milk I've ever tasted.

Allan quietly added, "I'll pass this time."

However, in a few months, Allan was back with us for more adventures at the dairy. The endless opportunities along with the earthy smell of cow manure and rotting straw energized us as we sought the freedom to be wild and creative in our play. Perhaps we'd figure out how to make parachutes out of our dads' handkerchiefs to see which carried the largest load. There was always something waiting for us to discover, all on our own. We were a unique generation: one with free time, unburdened with tasks and chores to help our families survive and before the revolution in technology. We planned, took risks, and made things while using our imaginations without relying too much on adult interventions. I wouldn't have had it any other way.

Chapter 16

THE DAY THE CRUSHERS RODE INTO TOWN

"Hey, did you see who's in town?" yelled Richard Kinchen when he reached the group assembled in front of the Frostie. He'd run down A Street and made a left turn at the parking lot in front of Dixon's only fast food restaurant. Like most of the guys in the parking lot, Rich wore a white T-shirt, blue Levi jeans that were a little short by current standards, and a pair of Converse All-Stars. His hair was curly but combed back with a sticky pomade. "I don't know where they're from, but there must be twenty cars."

Nothing created an electric buzz more than hearing of an out-of-town car club cruising the streets of town, especially if it was a full club. In 1962, the California car club culture had swept the state after exploding to attention in Southern California in the years after the War. Although car clubs had existed before then, the return of hundreds of thousands of soldiers, sailors, and marines provided the flammables needed to spread the movement throughout California and then the nation. Car clubs existed in most medium sized towns and small cities. A decade or so later, George Lucas made Modesto famous for its large and thriving car club culture when he made the cult classic movie, *American Graffiti.* Sometimes, if I had nothing to do and my homework was done, I'd head downtown where teenagers hung out. This usually meant the Frostie. where high school students and the under-20 crowd lucky enough to have cars parked and sipped sodas, ate soggy fries, and chewed thin hamburgers heavy with sweet pickle relish. Those a little older even smoked cigarettes and tried to look like James Dean. My friends and I were too young to drive cars or smoke cigarettes, so we hoped we could hang out without being teased or bullied by the older guys. We kept a low profile and only spoke when spoken to.

"Where are they from?" someone yelled back. "Are they local?" We all knew the reputations of car clubs in larger towns near us like the Woodland Coachmen, Vacavillians, and the Davis Accelerators. At the time, I was so tall and I wasn't very heavy so if it was the notorious Coachmen, I'd find more homework to do. If they were coming, quietly slipping away was probably the best idea until I had the body mass necessary to hang around a little longer. I knew the benefits of discretion and was willing to exercise my options.

"I don't think they're from around here," Rich said as he caught his breath. Just then we sighted the lead car in the club run moving east toward the Frostie. It was a '56 Chevy Impala with four rather large guys staring in our direction. They wore matching lightweight jackets with the collars pulled up. Two of the guys wore their hair in a flat top and fins with the top short but pushed up with pomade and the sides long and combed back. The other two riders wore the more traditional flat top with no fins.

More cars followed the leader. Each car seemed to be a different year and was custom painted. There were also '57, '58, '59, and '61 Chevys painted a variety of bright candy apple red or other metallic colors. Several of the Bucket T and cut-up Willys with chopped bodywork that lifted and eliminated body sections were painted with flames stretching out from the engine to the back side of the car. A few "street rods" had side chrome pipes. Most rode on customized chrome rims and wide tires. I stood in awe as car after car passed. The loud engines made the quiet street in small-town America sound an airport, as drivers revved their engines.

Tim Millans, who stood nearest the street finally got close enough to read a stamped metal plaque in a back window. "It says Lodi Crushers," he yelled our way.

During the time the cars drove by and "hard looks" and long stares were exchanged, a few guys in the Frostie's lot were yelling that reinforcements were needed. "Has anybody seen LeRoy Brinkfield or Charlie Fangio?"

Butch Serrano said he would try to find Peter Solista.

The group at the Frostie didn't include the hometown bad boys, who liked to brawl and give a tough-guy attitude and who knew how to back it up 100%. I guess we felt threatened, but we instantly felt included in a group that was being threatened, even if no contact had occurred. Butch took off in an effort to find reinforcements. Street lore spoke about motorcycle and car clubs that rode into smaller communities and virtually took over the drive-ins, major street corners, or even entire towns, like Hollister in 1947. So why did I hang around? Curiosity? I don't know, but this was my group, and we meant to protect our place.

Tensions were still running high when the club circled back and drove menacingly near those still leaning casually against the few cars that remained parked at the Frostie. Few of these cars had any street credibility, and most were basic unmodified cars that kids used to go to and from school or borrowed to go study at the local Carnegie Library. Overall, we looked pretty wimpy. Then I saw a passenger riding in a 1961 Pontiac painted in a sparkling blue. It looked like my cousin, Leon Tetz, who lived in Lodi. Leon was my age, and he was what we described as a "big boy." He was physically big and his dirty blond hair was combed back and sported a falling curl over the top part of his forehead.

Leon? It never crossed my mind that Leon was in Dixon or belonged to a car club for that matter. The Tetz family had moved from North Dakota when I was 10. I liked them. We visited the Tetz's often when we went to Lodi.

We never saw the Crushers again. They took off after their second run through town. When I saw Leon in Lodi a few weeks later, he explained that the Crushers had heard there was a big dance in Dixon, and they went to check it out. They weren't impressed by what they saw in town and left.

As I considered this chance encounter, I concluded the whole incident was stupid. Sports and athletic contests were so much more sensible. We almost had a physical altercation between people who didn't know each other and who might have actually had a lot in common. The youth-inspired car clubs disappeared and were replaced by white-haired old men socializing with their wives at car shows, and the type of tribalism exhibited that night faded away and left in the dust of the middle 20th century. I assumed petty tribalism was gone forever. I was wrong.

Chapter 17

THE END OF THE SEASON

I heard voices but couldn't track their meaning. I looked straight up into the night sky and barely made out the faint stars through the strong artificial light pushing back the darkness. Then I heard someone yell, "Are you alright?"

I was momentarily confused and then I saw a man's face leaning down looking into mine. He was wearing a black ball cap and his long-sleeved shirt was stripped black and white. An excruciating pain was gradually taking over all my sensory functions.

I looked down to where the pain was exploding and invading my consciousness. My wrist made my arm look like the neck of a swan. It bent down and then curved up awkwardly. I felt like I was alone in some kind of bubble. I heard distant noises and voices but couldn't process much. Then there was Coach Yelle asking me, "Danny, can you hear me? Are you okay?" His hand clasped around my shoulder pads and he looked concerned but not alarmed.

I instinctively answered, "Yeah, I'm fine." But something was wrong and then... My arm. What happened? It was broken or something, and it wasn't good.

After a minute or two, I was helped up and led off the field. I don't know who took me to the sidelines for I still wasn't tracking very well. I heard someone say, "He must be in shock or have a concussion." I was pulled to a back bench where I sat unsteadily trying to clear my head. In a short time, I realized that I had been injured on a running play as we struggled against the bigger and stronger Galt team. They had been ahead by two touchdowns, and we were desperately trying to make it a closer game. So what happened to me? I had no memory of the play that caused my injury.

In those days, the town's only doctor, Dr. Price, attended all home football games to administer to injuries or any emergencies. Dr. Price had been my doctor for as long as I could remember. Occasionally, he visited our home when my sister or I were sick. My parents were always concerned when we came down with a flu or respiratory illness. Dr. Price was thin, wore glasses, and always looked a few hours short of a good sleep. His clothes were routinely rumpled and his shoes scuffed. His voice was quiet and always calming. I don't think I ever saw him without his fat, black leather bag; most community doctors carried one in those days.

My wrist was gently wrapped and he fashioned a sling. Dr. Price made plans for me to meet him at his downtown office where he would give me a shot for the discomfort. He said it would make me feel better, but my wrist radiated pain to my upper arm. I was then sent to the area's only hospital at the Woodland Clinic.

I remember walking down the shiny hallways in my football uniform. I felt foolish. The sense of being in a bubble was gone, and I was very much aware of my surroundings. I sensed that people were staring at me. Why not? It's not often that a young man in a grass-stained football uniform is seen walking inside a building even if it is a hospital.

The doctor met us and examined my arm. I must have had an X-ray or two but that memory is missing. What I do remember is the doctor talking to a nurse and asking her to hold my upper arm and shoulder area. He then said something like, "This may hurt for a minute or two." Fine. I had no idea what was coming next. He took hold of my hand and pulled. I don't know if I yelled, but I remember that I was struck with a searing pain that lasted some time longer than a minute, although the worst part lasted only 30 seconds or so. I was then fitted with a hard cast and sent home.

On Monday, the team typically met in the coach's classroom to watch game films and analyze what worked well or failed during the game. Players always looked forward to watching themselves and their friends on the large pull-down screen. In those days, television replay was unknown and a chance to watch football on a screen with stop action or slow motion was mostly unheard of.

As we moved closer to the play where I had been hurt, teammates and friends were saying things like, "Rott, I bet you really laid a lick on the guy you were blocking."

No one else remembered the play either. "I can hardly wait, Rott. Let's see what caused that broken arm. How about the other guy? Oh, this is going to be good."

Finally, we arrived at the play we were all waiting to watch. The ball was snapped. I moved quickly from my stance and began blocking my man. Just as suddenly, he thrust my head into the ground. I turned over onto my back. Then John McNaughton, the big tackle playing next to me, slowly moved forward. His assignment was to block the player in front of him but he was too slow. He tripped and fell violently on top of me. There it was on film. My lumbering teammate falling like a giant tree, snapping my wrist on a play where I was the only person he touched. The groans, laughs, hoots, and yells in the coach's classroom must have been heard down the hallway in both directions. I was immediately hit with a flying towel while poor John was punched in the shoulder and showered with crumpled paper and a towel or two. Some people describe this as male bonding, but at that moment, I wished I'd been somewhere else. I didn't play football until the next season and never lived down the great anticlimax of watching myself being mauled and having my wrist broken by my own teammate.

Chapter 18

THE TRIP TO CHICO STATE

The year we graduated high school, 1966, Jimmy Jones owned a 1957 Chevy hardtop, the car every kid wanted back in the late 50s and early 60s. Although not customized with chrome rims and a candy apple paint job, it was admired for being a clean stock model.

"Hit it," I said as I piled into the back seat, feeling every bit as liberated as any teenager taking a trip with friends for a day away from home. Jimmy had picked up Ronnie, who was riding shotgun. An adventure was about to begin for three small-town 17-year-old seniors from Dixon with a "free" day from the choking confinement of high school. "I can't wait to get out of here." We knew everything and felt nothing but our own invincibility.

That spring Ronnie, Jimmy, and I decided to visit a campus on a "senior skip day" for those seniors planning to attend college.

"We earned a day and we're not wasting it. Besides, my cousin said Chico State has wild women and lots of parties," Jimmy announced, which was all the convincing we needed to decide on our skip day target. No one seemed to care that we had already made a tentative commitment to a college recruiter representing a school in Idaho.

The three of us played football together and had been classmates since 1st grade. According to the custom of the day, we were known by our name ending in the "y" sound: Ronnie, Jimmy, and Danny. Almost everyone had names like Ricky, Bobby, Eddie, Larry, Charlie, and Tommy.

Ronnie Garcia was a well-muscled son of Spanish immigrants from Andalusia who had settled land around Winters and Dixon to farm peach and walnut orchards. Jimmy Jones's family had settled early in California by the 1880s and homesteaded land in the Tremont region south of Davis and a little north of Dixon. They operated a typical family farm of the day, much smaller than today's corporate farms. My family had arrived in 1953 and were never quite considered locals.

We headed north, talked sports, and sang songs with the AM radio blaring. The sound wasn't too clear and we were lucky to know a few of the words. Finally, we arrived in Chico and quickly found the Chico State College campus.

"Man, I can't believe this." I stammered. "They can't do this every day. Oh, man. Look at this." I was getting that gone-to-heaven glow. A special feeling of bewilderment charged through my body as I looked around.

An elaborate 1850 village stood in front of the Administration building and it included at least two Mississippi-style paddle wheel steamers. Hundreds of students, some clad in elaborate costumes of early America, walked, danced, and did snake line trots in front of the school.

"What the heck?" I kept repeating. On one paddle wheeler, a platform allowed for a dozen students room to stage a rousing dance and song routine. Although it was only noon on a Thursday, I could swear that several performers were drinking beer out of wooden mugs. Period-perfect store fronts, bars, barber shops, funeral parlors, and log cabins filled in the gaps. I smiled and shook my head. Several "lumberjacks" passed us singing a bawdy college drinking song that was new to us. We laughed and thought it quite hilarious.

Later we learned that for one week, campus organizations competed in friendly fashion to get their candidate elected Sheriff or Little Nell of Pioneer Days. Each group selected its own costumed theme and designed a storefront that fit. To win, they held parties, developed dance routines, learned songs, and generally tried to convince other students their efforts should be rewarded with a huge win over all other groups. Western life was portrayed accurately and with humor. The general student body determined the winner by ballot. The teamwork and preparation were immense. The costumes and pioneer city built on campus were of the highest quality work. It was a stunning display of energy, innovation, and cooperative effort.

Somewhere along the way as we walked around the campus soaking up the energy and general good nature of the event, we decided to tell people that we were freshmen enjoying our first Pioneer Week.

"We really like Alpha Chi sorority," I smiled and tried to look as cool as possible in front of the girls manning a booth in front of a saloon. They pretended to like us too as they told us that they loved freshman boys. They smiled and remarked that they would be at the Lambda Pi party later that night. There would be many kegs of beer and a live band playing on the roof of the garage. Apparently, Lambda Pi had ordered 30 kegs of beer and the orchard in the back of their house made the perfect location for a Pioneer Week party.

On the way home, I sat back, smiled, and let out a deep breath and proclaimed, "I'm going to Chico State next year."

Ronnie and Jimmie looked at each other and shrugged. They had made up their minds and weren't going to be distracted and change direction now. Farm people I know tend to be that way.

Two years later my friends were on their way home to Dixon from Idaho for the Thanksgiving holiday when they hit black ice and the '57 Chevy hardtop flipped over and was totally wrecked. No one was seriously hurt but that beautiful Chevy would take part in no new stories or adventures.

I thrived at Chico State and graduated in four years but stayed two more years taking Master's classes. I met interesting people from all parts of California. Some of my best friends were from high schools that had been rivals just a few years earlier. Chico was just what I needed to open up and become a little more sociable. Years later when I told stories of life during college, I referenced the cult classic movie "Animal House" and smiled as the John Belushi character appeared in my mind's eye at the Lambdi Pi house shouting, "Toga, toga, toga!" What a trip it all turned out to be.

Chapter 19

THE LAST TIME I SAW DARRYL

The pick struck the hard, dry clay making it difficult to hold onto the handle. Thunk. The sound was like an ax striking a hollow log, but I didn't slow down or look up. In my personal fantasy, the Russians were watching, and they didn't stop because it was beginning to get hot: just the opposite. California in July heats up as early as 8 am. At 8:30 the trench I was digging was now at least five yards long and five feet deep. Developing a rhythm helped ward off fatigue and it was important our adversaries saw that young Americans were strong and tough enough to withstand the menace posed by the worldwide communist threat.

My partner, Patrick Kilkenny, was a tall muscular redhead whose large extended family had immigrated to Dixon before the start of the 20th century. I liked working with Patrick because of his physical strength and endurance. He was two years older, and I always thought he set a good example for me as we worked a summer job as laborers for the school district. We were lengthening the trench that connected the district office to the main city sewer pipe not knowing that life for me was about to change for the worse.

"Danny, here comes your dad." Patrick startled me. I stopped suddenly, almost in mid- swing. Now I looked up and saw my dad slowly walking through the school parking lot, moving in our direction. Dad was a long strider but today he seemed to be walking against a nonexistent wind.

"What's he doing here?" I mumbled to myself. "Dad never talks to me during working hours. Wonder what's going on?" He wasn't wearing his customary suit that he wore every day school was in session. In the summer, he wore slacks, a nice shirt, and a fedora to shade his partially balding head from the sun. I rarely saw him even though I had a job as a school district maintenance helper, making $1.75 an hour during the summer months. We did everything, including jobs that required hard labor. In 1966, I was fortunate to have a regular part-time summer job to save money for college expenses.

"Danny, I need to talk to you for a minute," he said in a hushed tone. "Hello, Patrick." He nodded in Patrick's direction.

I jumped out of the trench and walked over to where he stood with his back to Patrick. "Hey, Dad. What's up?" I asked cautiously.

"I've got some bad news." He looked directly into my eyes. He was good at that when he had something serious to discuss. Maybe it was his training as a chief petty officer in the Navy during the war years or his years as a school administrator, but I knew that this look, at this moment, required my full attention. "Darryl was killed last night in an accident out on Tremont Road. I've been told that he was thrown from a car and the impact caused serious damage to his heart. A group of friends were out in the country fooling around in cars and there was an accident."

"That can't be," I stuttered. "I saw him last night on my way home from summer basketball." I knew my dad was right, but I protested. "It's not true. He's fine." He had to be. He was my best friend and had been since third grade.

"I'll see you tonight or later today if I learn something new." Dad walked head down back to his office.

I slowly returned to where Patrick was taking a break waiting for me and told him what I had learned. I was dazed. Hadn't I seen Darryl last night? He was the last person I spoke to on my way home. He was sitting in Mike Bertucci's car. Mike was three years older than us and a junior at Chico State College. Friendly and outgoing, Mike helped his father farm his almond orchards. He made enough money to go to college and buy a new 1965 Chevelle Super Sport painted candy apple red. Around town, he wasn't known to be a wild or reckless kid. What did Darryl say? "We're meeting some girls. We scored a six pack of Coors. Do you want to go?"

"Nah," I'd responded. "I have to work tomorrow. I'll see you this weekend."

A six pack of beer? A beer a piece? It didn't make sense.

Patrick and I went back to work although my work fantasy about the Russians didn't slide back into my head to help me dull the monotony and low-level physical pain, a technique I used regularly. Instead, I thought about Darryl and what might have transpired after I went home. Darryl's dead? What did that mean? I wasn't sure, and I wouldn't know for a long time. I had never known anyone my age who died.

I thought about Darryl. His family had moved to California from Canada after the war, and his dad worked on the large Curry Ranch north of town as a farm mechanic. They lived for years on the ranch in a small house with his mom, dad, two brothers, and a sister. His mom was an ethnic Finn and had the largest blue eyes I had ever seen as did all four children. In fact, his sister was nicknamed "Owl Eyes." Besides having the family's large blue eyes, Darryl had curly blond hair and wide pink cheeks. I always wondered if all Finns had large blue eyes and pink cheeks.

Eventually the family moved to Dixon and bought a house on West F across the street from us where we lived together like family for many years. Darryl was a happy, even-tempered, and thoughtful friend. Similar traits and values ran in the family. I often had lunch and even dinner at the Kleebergers. Mrs. Kleeberger seemed to have enough for me and often invited me to stay and share their food.

Later, I was told that this was a bizarre accident. Mike's car hit a pothole in the road, and Darryl's door flew open. He was ejected. No one was wearing a seatbelt. They didn't find him for 15 minutes. Except for the door, Mike's car sustained no visible damage. This was my introduction to the fact that life is unpredictable. I thought and wrote about this incident many times trying to make sense of the tragedy. I still don't understand except that sometimes unfair events shake our confidence without notice or mercy. The older I got, the more times I was reminded of this theme.

PART TWO

College Years

Chapter 20

THE ACTOR AND ME

During the summer of 1970, I ran into a friend from Dixon who had also enrolled at Chico State.

"Hey, Rott. I just got a part in a new movie being made in Vacaville. Why don't you come down to Veterans Hall where they're hiring movie extras and I'll get you on?" Bobby "Roberto" Machado was one of those kinds of guys everyone knows who can talk their way into a Royal Coronation and sit next to the king. Bobby patiently explained how he had been selected to play a minor part in a new Jon Voight movie entitled "The All American Boy" being filmed in Vacaville. He had taken boxing at Chico State and even fought a couple of times on the college team against Cal and Stanford. Jon Voight would play the nation's new "white wonder" and Bobby would "bob and weave" at the gym for effect in the background. Who knows what he had told the film's producer about himself.

During high school, I joined the Drama Club and was selected for a big part in each of my four years. I liked acting. As a freshman, I hit the gold standard when I had a full-frontal kissing part with Mary Mince, a popular senior and head cheerleader. I was convinced that my acting days peaked when I graduated from high school.

In a short time, I was selected as a movie extra, which expanded my theatrical experiences for several days at $13.20 a day, minus union dues. I think I was hired because I had a summer job requiring short hair and no sideburns. The story was set in straight-laced 1961 small-town America. Evidently it was difficult at that time to find young people who didn't have facial or long hair. The other positive in my favor was that everyone on the crew seemed to know "Roberto" by name, and they all behaved as if he were part of management. They didn't seem to realize that he was a college student from Dixon. Bobby was one smooth talker.

We met on the movie set in the golden hills north of Vacaville. In summers the hills are hot, dry, and full of star thistle that stabs through socks and settles in small voids between shoe and sock. At that point, fingers are not effective in removing them. The only word that describes the rest of the day was "torture."

The shade available, a scattering of heritage oaks, seemed to be allocated to the full-time movie crew. Each day the temperature hit at least 100°. Movie extras lined up last for drinks of water. Convenient plastic water bottles were still unknown, and hats weren't permitted as they didn't fit in with the scenes being filmed. I had also made a ridiculous decision to wear a blue coat each day so that I would be able to easily identify myself as a member of the crowd when I saw the finished movie after its release. The heat beat down on cast and crew, especially those extras who played the part of townspeople.

"They're looking for someone to play the movie double for Jon Voight," Bobby announced on the second day of shooting. "I told them you'd be perfect. You look like his brother except you're taller. I'll see what I can do." Knowing Bobby, anything was possible. At that point, I had only seen Jon Voight from a distance on the set.

During the course of the next few days, Bobby dropped by to give me encouraging updates about my chances of becoming Jon Voight's double. "Don't worry. I'm working on it." he said confidently.

However, I spent most of my time on the movie set standing around, not at all like the next step up in acting that I'd anticipated. Then on the last day, things changed. Bobby told me that I didn't have the union card necessary to be a movie double, but he was working on something big and would return shortly.

When he returned, he had a big grin.

"So what's the story?" I asked.

"Follow me and wear this." He handed me a red badge held together by a white lanyard. I placed it around my neck. We headed down to a restricted area, past uniformed security guards and to a flat section of land where four or five trailers were parked. Bobby walked up to a trailer and knocked on the door. Out stepped Jon Voight. My eyes must have gotten big like slapstick comedians of the 1930s like Stan Laurel of Laurel and Hardy. Jon Voight laughed.

We spent 10 or 15 minutes talking, mostly about sports and the hot California weather with our dry climate. We took a few photos and I shook his hand. The movie, which also starred Anne Archer, bombed and didn't get much national distribution so the highlight of my acting career remained a kiss in a school play. Nevertheless, I did get to meet a talented actor.

Chapter 21

THE SUMMER JOB PRANK

"Mom, hurry. See if Dad has any of those knee-high white socks. I can't find any that are long enough. I've got to get to work by 2.," I was yelling and in a panic.

"Okay, hold your horses. I'll look again." Mom went back into their bedroom and finally came out with a pair of white socks that Dad wore with Bermuda shorts. They were longer than anything I had.

I needed to get to my summer job at the Standard station on the freeway at the Coffee Tree side of Interstate 80 near Vacaville. On a three-day weekend like the Fourth of July, Friday afternoon promised to be crazy. This was my second summer working at the gas station, and I was prepared for anything. I had to get there on time, and I was running late.

We wore a uniform: blue pants, white shirt with a Chevron logo on the right side of the chest, and a folding blue cap similar to those worn by off-duty American Army soldiers during WW ll. Special black shoes with thick rubber soles that resisted petroleum product damage and slippage on concrete were also required. Standard stations furnished the uniforms so that all station employees were dressed exactly the same. They were delivered weekly to the station in a sealed plastic wrap with our names smartly labeled for easy identification. Our dirty uniforms were collected by the same delivery driver and taken to be cleaned and the cycle continued exactly the same each week.

"Mom, this uniform is all goofed up and doesn't fit. The pants are too short or something and my socks don't cover my legs," I complained before leaving home. At 6 foot 5, I was too tall to borrow or trade with anyone else.

"You'll make do this one time. Use Dad's socks. Now scat."

I ran to my car. The job helped me maintain my car, which my dad bought me when I passed my sophomore year of college. He was very proud and also grateful because he didn't want me to get drafted and sent to Vietnam.

"Hey, where's the flood?" yelled Allan Haight after I arrived at the station and he pointed at my too-short pants. I had joined many of my Dixon friends who were going to college and working for Standard in 1968. These were union jobs paying $3.65 per hour for a straight eight-hour shift. We took lunch if time allowed. I made over $3,000 a summer living at home so that almost everything I made was saved. Tuition was $99 a semester, twice a year, and my room cost $40 per month. This was a pretty fair deal, I thought. My parents helped out when I needed help.

I rolled up my sleeves as they too were a little short. Others joined in mocking me for looking "goofy" in the poorly fitting uniform. "Hey, Mortimer Snerd, where's Charlie McCarthy?" snorted Ricky Sequeira as he gave a high-pitched laugh and walked off to pump gas for an arriving customer. Another guy asked if I was trying out for a cornfield scarecrow.

The cost of gas hovered between 24 cents to 34 cents a gallon during the summers I worked. At these gas stations, no one was permitted to stand around with nothing to do. If there was only one car getting gas, it was not unusual to have three employees pumping gas, washing the windows, checking air pressure, and showing the customer the dip stick so they knew the status of the oil in the engine. Customers loved the attention.

Since this was July 4, a huge holiday getaway, the station was Central Valley hot and busy as a disturbed ant hill. A few customers from the Bay Area refused to roll down their windows more than a couple of centimeters, just enough to push or punch a credit card out the window while keeping their air conditioning on. We needed to get on our hands and knees to retrieve the cards to run them through the station's credit card machine.

"Good afternoon, Ma'am. Fill your tank today?' I said this so often on busy days that I dreamed it over and over as I tried to get to sleep at night. I didn't mind these busy days when there was usually only time to get a coke or bottle of water. I missed lunches and often didn't stop moving from the start to finish of my shift. I made more money than other people my age who didn't work union jobs, which made the hard work worth it. I always thought it better to be busy than bored. "Stop in and see us again."

Occasionally Standard Oil regional managers stopped by without introducing themselves and monitored our efforts and interactions with customers. If we had left our hat at home or were not repeating the accepted greeting and closing, we might be fired or blackballed for the next summer. These managers hammered the theme that we sold service.

At the end of a grueling day with temperature that flirted with 100, my shift ended. The new shift that worked from 10 p.m. to 6 a.m. arrived. As I turned to walk slowly back to my car, I noticed David Bonillo getting out of his car. David was 5'7" and a pudgy 200 pounds. His uniform pant legs were rolled up at least six to eight rolls. The arm length of his white shirt hung loosely and covered his hands.

I immediately shot a glance at Allan and Ricky, who were near their cars and rolling on the ground in laughter. Earlier in the week, they had intercepted the uniform shipment and changed name tags for David's and my uniform bundle with an artful slice of an exacto-knife. They then carefully resealed them with clear tape.

We had fun and worked hard, but it was worth it. There was a sense of self-worth and accomplishment. We wanted to go to college, and we earned most of our expenses. Today, the average student graduates with a $30,000 debt hanging like a dark cloud over their start into the workforce. A recent article indicated that half of all college students eat one to two meals a day and go to school hungry. I can't say our experiences made us better people, but I am convinced that we started our adult life with a bit more work experience and more optimism than today's kids.

Chapter 22

THE DIXON WATERING HOLE

"Are you sure it will get me into the bar? I can't afford to get caught and busted. You're working and everyone we know will be in Dawson's since it's Friday afternoon. I have to see what's going on." Allan and I were both living at home again for summer to save money for college.

He squinted and smiled. "We look pretty close, almost like brothers. We both have blond hair. Good enough." In 1969, many of our friends from high school were 21 and had reached the magic threshold dreamed about by those not yet there.

I walked into Dawson's Bar and sat down. "Hey, what's going on? Anybody want a beer?" What a rookie mistake for someone my age to utter at a bar. At least five guys raised a hand, downed their beer, and clanked an empty glass on the bar.

The bar tender quickly moved in our direction, too quickly, in my estimation. He was thin, short and looked to be in his mid-50s. His brown hair was neatly combed over from right to left and held in place with a light application of pomade. He wore a white, long sleeved shirt with both the neck and sleeves buttoned tight. His most prominent feature was a pair of coke-bottle thick glasses. Behind the lenses his eyes appeared large and his skin lighter than the rest of his face. I felt that my attempt to pass on Allan's ID faced an imposing challenge. He looked my way and mumbled, "So who's the big winner?" The man behind the glasses asked no questions.

In my best impersonation of a movie tough guy, I threw a $20 bill on the shiny dark wooden bar. I made no eye contact and acted as if I had done this hundreds of times. I turned to listen to the latest joke being told and patiently waited. The next time I turned around to peek, my change was laid out with coins topping the bills. I wasn't sure whether I should take the change immediately or leave it on the bar for all to see.

Dawson's Cigar Store began business in Dixon in 1908 when 18 bars fiercely competed for the town's 300 people. Farming and ranching were labor intensive and ranchers and farmers flooded into town to wet their whistles. Dawson's survived when all of the other watering holes disappeared like leaves falling when the delta breezes blew into town off the Carquinez Straits. I knew many ranchers, farmers, young men, and characters frequented Dawson's, which had become an institution with a 90-year history as little changed in the interior. "Hey young fella, haven't seen you in here before. I know almost everyone in Dawson's. I've been farming for 50 years between here and Davis. Carl Becker's the name, with a B, not a P," the man said quickly with a smile on his face.

"I'm Danny Rott. My family are newcomers and moved here in 1953," I said trying hard not to laugh. A large hand immediately moved in my direction.

"Glad to meet ya," said Mr. Becker with a B, not a P.

I'm tall but not *farmer big*. His hand dwarfed mine and I immediately thought of my Grandma Johnson's large hand fashioned from a half century of milking cows in Norway and Minnesota. Then I felt searing pain as my hand was squeezed until I thought a bone was going to break. Just when I thought I might yell, it stopped.

A few of my friends laughed. Bobby Giannoni, a friend of mine, who worked with his dad farming east of town said, between hiccup-like laughs, "Don't ever shake hands with Carl Becker. Ever. He loves to catch people off guard. He's a good guy but with an odd sense of humor and he's very strong."

As I let myself relax, I looked around and noticed several dirty spittoons tucked under the bar railing. Trophy deer heads lined the back wall behind the bar as well as a stuffed pheasant or two. While making a trip to the rest room, I noticed an open room with round tables and a group of locals finishing a game of cards. Most of the card games were held in the morning after the ranchers, buyers, and farmers had completed local business deals. Occasional games started before heavy drinking on Friday and Saturday evenings. Stories around town spoke of more millionaires playing poker than other players, although they couldn't be identified because everyone dressed the same in collared work shirts, blue jeans, and boots

I comfortably sat back on the railing with my third beer listening to the tenth big story of the night. Tom Galindo, another high school classmate, was telling the story about Bobby and the riding lawn mower. "Yeah, he was out at the Farmer's Invitation Only Reception at the John Deer dealership. I'm sure he was feeling no pain enjoying free drinks, when he decided to try out a sit-down riding mower. Well one thing led to another. He started it and drove eight blocks on First Street and then turned at the corner of A Street and drove straight into Dawson's."

Then I thought I heard a whistle. Mild curiosity caused me to turn my head slightly. I saw one of my dad's best friends, Jim Kilkenny, looking directly at me. We knew each other well. He was good friends with the owners and was the long time Post Master. He and his wife Claire had been to our house the night before for dinner with my folks. My cloak of anonymity disappeared. *Not good,* I thought. He pointed to the front door. I smiled, nodded my head, said goodbye to my friends, and walked out onto the sidewalk at the corner of A and First smiling at my small adventure. *At least I didn't get busted with Allan's ID.* After leaving, I walked down the street disappeared into the night. Eventually, the original Dawson's did too.

Chapter 23

THE BIG DOWNTOWN BUST

"Put your hands on the top of the car and don't make a move or I'll take the dog out and you won't like that." In the background I heard loud, angry barks and growls from a huge German Shepherd. He wasn't more than a couple of feet from me and I knew he meant business. I saw his big white teeth out of the corner of my eye. His eyes were huge and bulging at the sockets. Allan Haight was already sitting in the back of the police car.

We were stopped on First Street next to the Carnegie Library. Dixon was still a small, sleepy town with only one stop light at the intersection of First and A. Five years earlier the city placed the light after the collision of a police car bringing Tom Sork through town on the way to the hospital after he was shot in a well-known hunting accident. LeRoy Cagle's car legally entered the intersection after making a stop but was T-boned by the police car driving at high speeds. By pure luck, no one was injured in that accident but the light went up soon after.

I was angry and bristling with defiance. "Why? We didn't do anything." I was almost shouting. "You have no right to stop us and make us do anything."

Allan was taking a more stoic approach to the situation we found ourselves in and complied and had gotten into the town's second patrol car without making a fuss. He assumed the role of observer to what surely qualified as a bad B movie script. He wasn't scared, but he shook his head and looked more than a little amused.

Just minutes before a patrol officer had signaled us to pull over. The patrolman then called his sergeant, Blake Bureford, a long-time member of the local police force who drove the only patrol unit containing a dog. When he arrived, he greeted us with, "What are you boys doing out at this hour? You do know it's one o'clock." He said it like we'd forgotten that one o'clock had some special meaning.

I explained that Bobby Machado had told us to meet him after his date with his girlfriend. I continued by saying that we had broken no laws and were cruising around until we made contact sometime between midnight and 1:00. We were going to make plans to go snow skiing the next day. This was a reasonable plan since there was no other way to make last-minute decisions like the one we were contemplating. Cell phones had not yet been invented. On this weekend, we were not expecting to work our holiday vacation jobs. What's more, driving around town in a car was a normal activity for people our age, especially at night. Stopping and talking to others doing the same thing was routine. Sometimes this meant talking to a car full of girls

Finally, I too got in the back of the patrol cruiser. The two officers talked quietly between themselves and Sergeant Bureford returned to the car. He leaned his head down in our direction. He was a big man over six feet tall and more than 200 hundred pounds. His head was big, round, and fleshy like he might have been an athlete at one time but age, a lack of exercise, and overeating had done him no favors. Had I done something wrong, I might have felt intimated, but his appearance at the door just made me angry. "You boys need to go home. This is your last chance." He did his best to give an impression of a Marine Corps drill sergeant.

"We didn't do anything. You can't make us go home without a reason," I heard myself saying. I was adamant. When I looked at Allan, he was rolling his eyes.

"Take them to the office, Patrolman," Sergeant Bureford told his partner. "I'll meet you there."

"Now what?" I thought.

Allan was shaking his head. "What do you think will happen now?" he asked as we drove the short distance to the police station.

This sort of thing didn't happen to two well-known local college students at home working to support their expenses. Allan and I had grown up in town. We played sports in high school. Allan played baseball and I played football and basketball. My dad was a local elementary school principal and Allan's farmed a small almond orchard east of town. Both dads had served in the Navy in WWII. This was unbelievable.

We ended up sitting in the police station for an hour or two before our parents were called to come and get us. Our dads were quiet and deferential to the police, who explained that we refused their legitimate request to go home. The only thing my dad said to me when we got home was, "Hey, knock it off," when I kicked the couch on the way in. I guess I was hoping for a more spirited defense of our position. In the morning, not much was said and I didn't want to talk to anybody at the house for a few days.

Sometimes when I watch the news concerning young people and the police, I remember this incident. I'm reminded of my reaction then and wonder what might have been if I wasn't white, well-known in a small town, and without so much as a blemish with law enforcement.

Mom on family farm in Minnesota.

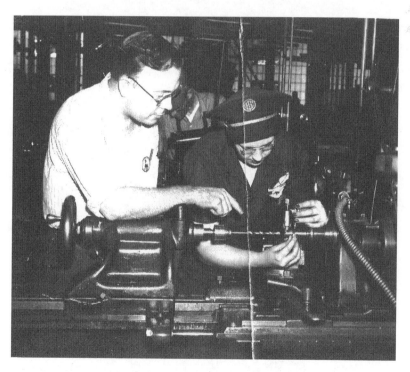

Mom being trained as a machinist.

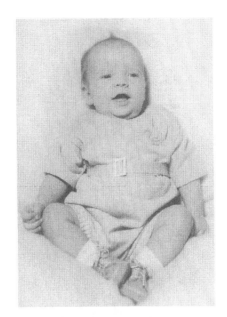

My baby picture.

Me in my baseball uniform.

My mom, Borghild "Bea" Rott.

My dad in his school office.

Me and my sister Dian with new bikes.

*Practicing my accordion before
a performance.*

Me: third from left.

My dad middle of hay wagon.

My dad Emer Rott 1935.

Dian and I on the road in 1958.

Dad at the North Dakota school house.

The barn at the Johnson farm.

Grandma playing the organ.

Me on tractor on farm in Minnesota.

Rick Carter, me, Dale Taylor at Dale's wedding.

Diana Green as a high school senior.

Aunt Irene.

Tom Sork as a high school senior.

Me: back row vertical striped shirt, cousin Steve: third from right kneeling.

Sequeira Dairy 60 years after the big egg fight, outside Dixon on Pedrick Road.

 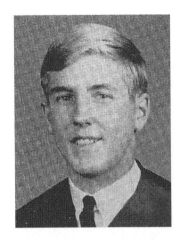

Ricky Sequeira as a high school senior.   *Allan Haight as a high school senior.*

Chopped Willys.

Cousin Leon Tetz as a high school senior.

Me, Bill Hull, Jim Rehrmann.

Pioneer Week at Chico State 1966.

Pioneer Week at Chico State 1966.

Darryl Kleeberger as a High
School Senior.

Roberto "Bobby" Machado.

Me and Jon Voigt on movie set.

Me and my Car.

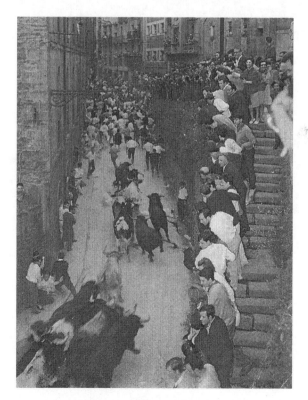

Running with the bulls 1973.

Running with the bulls 1973.

Bill Paterick, me, Harry Axhelm.

Me and students.

Joan and I shortly after we were engaged.

Tara and Ivan parasailing.

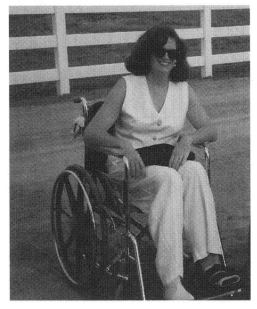

Joan recovering from ankle injury.

Aud, Suzanna, and Kijel.

Last photo taken of Suzanna.

Ivan and I show off our agates.

Tara, Ivan, Erik and I hunt for agates on the beach.

Agates found on the beach, note the variety of color and size.

Dian 1978.

Mom, Joan, and I at the memory home.

Xochilt Quitegua and I.

Me with Sadie, Ivan with Indy at Trinidad rental.

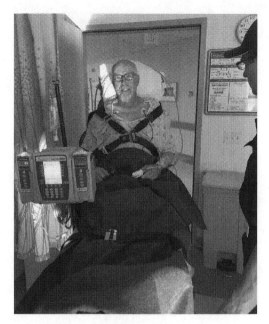

Me in the ambulance after heart attack.

TV's in rooms on second floor.

Main entrance to the Sniff Hotel Portland, Oregon.

Hunspach church.

Annmarie, Rudi, Briggitte, and I.

Joan, Ivan, Aud, Sammy, and I at Auds home in Herns, Hedmark, Norway.

Norwegian mountain mushrooms.

Joan and I hiking a glacier in Norway.

Chapter 24

THE NIGHT THE STREET CLAPPED

Slap, clap, slap, clap, slap, clap. *What the heck is that?* I thought. Clap, clap, clap. A slow rhythmic noise sounded down the street and as I looked left I saw them coming. At least fifty riot clad sheriff's deputies dressed in hard helmets, holding long dark clubs, wearing black boots with the pant legs tucked inside marched in my direction. I froze. Sure, I had seen images on TV news and in the papers, but I'd never observed a contingent of riot police on the move. As they came closer, I noticed that they were also slapping their riot sticks into the other hand for effect. I thought I had experienced adrenalin rushes when I played high school football but this was an off-the-charts experience. Clap, clap, clap, clap. The sound bounced off the pavement and echoed down the street. This was happening in Chico?

The mid-60s were one of the most tumultuous periods in American history. Huge social changes and an unpopular war in Vietnam created an unstable, raucous, and sometimes violent time. Many young people demonstrated against the war, for racial equality and more personal freedom. Protests and marches for change and an immediate end to the war were an almost daily occurrence. During most of that time, I was comfortably situated in a relatively safe environment in a small college originally chartered as a teacher training facility serving Northern California. Chico State College had a well-known reputation as a laid-back, isolated college that put friendly social interaction at a high priority.

As time went on, that started to change and we began to realize that we were not immune to the activities rocking the rest of the country. We listened to the music of the day and were close enough to San Francisco that the whiff of the Summer of Love moved our way. Music, drugs, and calls for freedom overtook our sunny bastion of self-indulgence. Growing up in a small northern California community without many of the experiences of my urban and Bay Area classmates, I was the proverbial "deer in the headlights." Timidly I peered out at a world seemingly out of control. I remember thinking quite often, *Now what?* I watched astonished as one after another of my friends succumbed to marijuana, Janis Joplin, and the Grateful Dead. Some were drafted into military service. I desperately kept my college deferment. My roommates and I liked college life. We bought a Santana album, placed speakers near our open front door and cranked it to obnoxiously loud levels. I guess we thought that was cool.

In early 1970, Chico too, was consumed with protest and confrontations between activist students on one side and the college administration, the City of Chico, and conservative students on the other. Life did go on, however and after a class I started talking to an attractive girl that I had been sitting next to often that semester. She dressed in a plain manner with a newer, natural style of the day including little makeup and long, straight hair. My impression was that she was shy and sensitive. Then she surprised me. "Would you like to come over to dinner tonight? My roommate went home for a few days and I feel like cooking." She then smiled. Her name was Diane Pichetti.

"Sure" I said. "That sounds great." After moving out of the dorms, my meals were usually sandwiches or a fast food burger. Besides, I didn't get an offer like that often from a girl as attractive as Diane.

This particular week had been designated as Survival Faire Week and each day students active in the Ecology Movement planned activities and projects in front of the school on First Street to show the dangers of air, land, and water pollution. I had no idea that one of the most famous events in the history of Chico State would take place that day and a confrontation between students and police was already boiling. Naturally, both sides had been watching, reading, and learning about what was happening around the nation.

My date with Diane was scheduled for 5. Chico was small and most students walked or rode bicycles. It didn't make sense to drive a car for short distances although a long-standing joke about one of my close friends was that he drove a block to school on more than one occasion. This and other whimsical thoughts crowded my head as I walked down the street on the way to the house Diane shared with her roommate. I skirted the campus and was passing one of the older residential neighborhoods that surrounded the campus. Each was a rental and they had a friendly vibe with students sitting on porches reading, talking or drinking beer. A block away from Diane's I heard the sound.

I rushed over to Diane's and knocked hurriedly and loudly at the door. She opened it and smiled.

"Diane. Come out and look. This is wild. Hurry."

She walked out on the porch and gazed in the direction I was pointing. She turned back to me and just stared.

"Can you believe this? Have you heard anything about what's happening?" I asked excitedly. "This is big".

"No, not really", she replied softly. There was no change in her demeanor, and she just looked at me while I was trying to soak up everything as the phalanx marched by and the noise ebbed and receded. There was absolutely no glimmer of interest from Diane. I realized that this was a problem. I didn't know what was happening, but I had to watch. I felt like a Labrador Retriever on the first day of hunting season. I barely kept my arms and hands still.

I finally ended up having dinner with her. To this day, I can't remember what I said or how I behaved. I couldn't concentrate or maintain a reasonable conversation. I finally made up an excuse for leaving early. I also remember the look on Diane's face and it wasn't a happy one. I couldn't help myself. I was pulled in the direction of the action outside.

I watched as police and students chased after one another throughout the dark night. Students made bonfires in the street to protest. Police and the fire department put them out. Evidently, sometime earlier in the day, a group of passionate students had decided they would close First Street as a symbolic act to bring the dangers of air pollution to the public's attention. How lighting bonfires throughout the night helped, I'm not sure. There was pushing and shoving between competing groups. Sixteen students and two professors were arrested on charges of conspiracy. Their actions were considered a felony by the district attorney. Most of the hundreds of students present gaped in wonder as Chico and the "Incident on First Street" became part of the wild and crazy Decade of Protest.

Later, with no one hurt, we all drifted downtown to drink beer, retell the night's stories, and attempt to make sense of the night's events and how we fit in. We would soon leave school, making our way into a fast-changing, if not, chaotic world as the Vietnam war came to an inglorious end.

Chapter 25

THE RUNNING OF THE BULLS

Packed to capacity, the bus slowly rolled into the small Spanish town of Pamplona, Spain. I had decided years before to attend the 1973 Festival of San Fermin held each year in July and experience an event that both excited and frightened me.

"We're here, mate," announced Rob, my traveling companion since we'd boarded the bus in Barcelona. Rob was from Glasgow, and like me, had arrived in Pamplona with only a backpack and a bad case of adventurism, and we both knew we hadn't come this far just to watch. The streets in Pamplona were typical: narrow and lined with older two -and three-story buildings with a smattering of street level markets, restaurants, and bars. On this special occasion, colorful flags and banners, primarily in red, outlined each street in the city center.

We quickly stored our backpacks with an enterprising Spaniard for a nominal sum and navigated into the large town square. Small tables and chairs were set up in almost every direction and the setting was similar to many of the older European towns I had visited, but today there were more people. The tables were full of revelers drinking wine or coffee. Men far outnumbered women. Many were wearing the traditional San Fermin uniform of white shirt, pants, and red scarf. A number of men were also wearing Spanish berets.

"Now what are we going to do?" I asked Rob, although I knew the question was somewhat rhetorical. "Let's walk around and see what else is here. Maybe we'll meet more English speakers and find out how this place works."

We arrived on July 7, one day after the festival officially kicked off.

I knew something about the event because I had read Hemingway's "The Sun Also Rises", and my best friends had attended the festival in 1970 when their parents gifted them money to backpack in Europe as a graduation gift. (My parents were not as forthcoming.) With big eyes and exciting stories, they recounted their experiences of running with the bulls. They explained how the bulls for the day's bullfight are run down a street and into the ring every morning of the festival at the sound of a cannon. Those present, and brave enough, run with the bulls and hope not to get knocked down, gored, or stepped on. Over a few beers, their tales seemed to grow and become more and more exciting.

As we walked Pamplona's streets, two major problems presented themselves. The first problem led to the second. As I navigated the crowded streets, I ran a gauntlet of Bota bags and bottles of wine. "Drink up," everyone seemed to say. Friendly Spaniards pulled me into small narrow wine bars. "Por favor, drink." I drank more wine in the first few hours in Pamplona than I had in my whole life up to that point. I was having fun AND this was a 24-7 activity that would last for the entire eight-day festival. The second problem was that the Spanish police tolerated no public drunkenness especially for those running with bulls each morning. To do so was foolish and dangerous to others. The Spanish police were very physical and carried long rubber truncheons that they didn't hesitate to use.

In spite of drinking wine all night, the adrenaline pumped hard through my body. Horns blew, people sang, and five-man marching bands snaked along cobblestone streets going nowhere in particular. I remember sharing wine with Scots, Irish, English, Swedes, as well as a few Americans. We laughed, philosophized, and promised each other that we would run and fear no bull. I built up the confidence I needed. "You can do this!" I shouted from time to time to no one in particular. Somewhere in the back of my head I remembered, *people die doing this.*

During the night heavy wooden boards were strategically placed between buildings and streets until all nonessential side streets were blocked off and one major street remained unimpeded. The 830-yard path from the outskirts of the city to the Plaza de Toros now awaited the annual tradition. Bulls fighting in the evening were run into the ring. Hundreds of thrill seekers took their places somewhere along the way and waited the day's run.

At exactly 7, a distant cannon boomed. Hundreds of white-clad participants reacted like they had been electrified. Some ran toward the bull ring and others seemed to jump and look quickly toward the boom while their feet pranced or moved nervously. I didn't feel drunk but I wasn't thinking clearly. I moved and jogged with those moving in the direction of the bull ring not knowing what to expect. Within just a few short minutes, dozens of runners turned a corner sprinting wildly in our direction. Soon after, a cow followed by bulls rounded the corner and two became five. I turned quickly and started running with fierce determination. The sound of thunderous hooves grew. I tripped and in one motion hit the street and crawled to the nearest building. I was terrified. Then it was over. The bulls had run past in seconds. I took my time getting up. Wow! What a rush!

"Did you run?" Rob asked. "I went back and slept in the park since I lost track of you and was in no shape to run. I'll go tomorrow for sure but I'll be more careful about what I drink," He sounded disappointed.

"Yeah. It's like stepping off a curb," I scoffed. He looked at me and we both started laughing. I told him what I remembered and we pledged to stay together until the next run. I then suggested, "I think we should start closer to the bull ring since the bulls are so fast. We can make it into the ring and not worry about being trampled."

We slept in the park and got up before dawn to take our places on the street. The spot was closer to the bull ring. The cannon sounded, and we ran like wild horses. As we made eye contact with the ring, we could hear people yelling and then hooves clomping the cobble stone street. I thought we would be in trouble when we arrived at the tunnel leading into the ring as everyone must funnel into the cave-like opening. We made it, and then my satisfaction turned to terror. Damn! Lining the ring were other runners who were packed against fences at least five to ten people deep. Now what? Someone screamed. I think it was me. The cows started through the tunnel. I put my head down and slammed into bodies pushed up against the walls. Then I noticed the bulls closely following the lead cows who were wearing noisy bells around their necks, something they are trained as calves to do. Both groups ran directly across the ring to an open gate on the opposite side, which was then promptly closed.

The next day I hitched a ride out of Pamplona with two girls driving a jeep heading back to Barcelona. Of course, I said, "I'll be back next year." That was almost 50 years ago. Rob stayed but I was exhausted and didn't think I could last one more day in a city where no one seemed to sleep and half of those awake drank, sang or danced all through the day and night.

Chapter 26

THE ESCORT

I tried to cope with a headache and muscle aches after sleeping on the train from Barcelona to Rome. I needed to reach the hostel and a real bed. At 24, I was backpacking in Europe. I hated leaving most destinations along the way, but time and funds were limited. Barcelona was one of those places that was so hard to leave. The artist Gaudi had used it as a canvas. Nearby in the pristine water of the Costa Brava, a few miles north of the city, vacationers from all over Europe galloped on the beach and into the ocean.

Suddenly I heard screams coming from the curving cobblestone sidewalk directly in front of me. A young well-dressed man was slapping a beautiful dark-haired lady. At one in the morning no one else was on the street. She staggered forward and received two kicks to her buttocks before stumbling into a doorway, quickly followed by the man. *"What the hell,"* I thought. And then they were gone.

I strolled out of the hostel the next morning onto the cobblestone of the in older neighborhood as the morning sun gently warmed my face. I heard a young woman's voice speaking perfect American English.

"Excuse, me. Are you an American?"

I slowly turned as I wasn't sure the question was intended for me. I had traveled nonstop from Barcelona the day before and had spoken very few times with English-speaking travelers. I was still tired and a bit confused by what I had seen the night before and had little time to become oriented to my surroundings. Standing near me was a young girl about my age and behind her was a group of seven or eight young women, who I figured were her traveling companions. After she had my attention, she asked, "Where are you going today?"

I shrugged, smiled, and said, "I'm not sure. Maybe the Coliseum."

"Can we go too?" she asked. She smiled, but her smile changed quickly to a worried, almost pleading look when I didn't answer immediately.

My answer was wrapped in a kind of bewilderment. "Sure. When were you leaving?"

"Whenever you are," she answered quickly. Her friends exchanged excited glances and quickly scurried to where we were standing. Most young adults dream of being irresistible to others their age, but this was ridiculous. Something told me this wasn't about me, but something that happened before I arrived that unnerved the group.

For the rest of the day my new traveling companions told me stories of being groped and harassed by young Italian men as they traveled across the city visiting historic and cultural landmarks. In some instances, young men offered to be guides or show the travelers around interesting parts of the city. Soon help and friendliness changed dramatically. Over-friendly doesn't describe what they experienced. "One guy grabbed my bottom and started rubbing his hand back and forth," explained the young women who had spoken to me first. Others briefly recounted how they had been touched on their breasts and body without warning. I recounted my story of the night before and my confusion about what had happened to the lady. I didn't know much about old world misogyny.

I also learned that many in the group didn't know each other but had connected in the hostel the night before, where they quickly became friends. Developing short-term relationships with fellow travelers was common among those backpacking through Europe. I too traveled with interesting groups from Scotland, Oregon, and an amusing group of French speakers from Quebec as we easily became travel friends. Their first night the young women developed a travel plan in the hostel lobby. The next morning, I emerged as the unsuspecting target.

The day unfolded at the Coliseum and other spots like the Spanish Steps. The fun sprouted like summer corn with a sense of adventure and constant chatter, growing as the group came together. It reminded me of family reunions I experienced when I was younger. Everyone shared personal histories and travel experiences as laughter erupted and the bond tightened between us. At the end of the day, we found a cheap Italian dinner recommended by a travel booklet. "So, where are we going tomorrow?" I asked sometime during one of our stops.

A sense of loss and disappointment struck as they spoke of heading out in a new direction. The Canadians were taking a train to Brindisi to board a ferry for Greece. An American group excitedly pointed north to Switzerland and the Alps. I never got used to these encounters when friends were made at times, for only a day. Both groups were pleased that they had had the opportunity to relax while visiting parts of Rome, as their fears subsided by traveling with a young countryman. I took a few photos. The people I met became memories. I determined the only thing to do was to start each new day fresh with a list of sights to see.

I left the hostel at a faster pace than the day before, but before I reached the corner to catch a bus, I heard, "Can we ask you a question? Are you sightseeing today?"

PART THREE

Career and Family

Chapter 27

THE POW TURNS TO TEACHING

Oh, Bill. Bill. BILL! The name rolled around my head like a loose bowling ball in a car trunk. *I can't believe you said that. Ah, geez...* I was blindsided and never expected a meeting to start like this.

The meeting began simply enough with Bill Paterick, a veteran fifth grade teacher, introducing himself and me to an assembled group of about 50 parents: both men and women. I stood up when introduced, smiled, and waved at those in attendance. Since this was a school on Travis Air Force Base, there were a number of men and women in dark green camouflage fatigues. I don't know what it is about fatigues, but they make people look bigger than when wearing civilian clothes.

As a new teacher hired in 1972, I was anxious to learn and become familiar with all aspects of my new job. I contacted staff and explained that I was interested in observing them, especially when it came to conferences with parents, especially in large meetings. I was excited to attend a meeting of 5th grade parents concerning the very sensitive topic of Human Growth and Development or Sex Ed. Bill welcomed the parents and told those assembled that he wanted to start off informally. Had I known what he had in mind, a sprint to the exit would have been in order.

Bill looked at the audience, smiled, and said, "You know, of course, that it's possible to get VD from a toilet seat." After waiting for that nugget to sink in, Bill finished by saying, "But it's a terrible place to take your date."

I froze and stared intently at the floor. I saw a small bug scurry across the light brown tile and wished I could do the same. Should

I get up and leave? Instead of increasing, my breathing slowed down as if to not draw any attention to myself. As I readied for the worst, chuckling and then louder laughing filled the small multipurpose room. I remember one woman's high-pitched cackle to this day.

Bill quickly began his formal presentation explaining the content of state-adopted Sex Ed curriculum and approved materials to be used. The program structure included Bill teaching boys while the girls were taught separately by Mrs. Brown, the school nurse. Mrs. Brown, who was also present, was a small, thin, almost mousy woman who looked very much the serious school nurse and someone students could look to for comfort away from home.

A short movie was shown giving more background information and explaining why the State of California felt it important to start providing students as young as 10 with this curriculum. The term *sex education* was never used at any time. Parents were then given time to ask questions and review or preview materials on a back table. Bill circulated and talked to parents individually or in small groups. His loud voice was heard over the din as well as his laugh, which seemed as regular as the click of a school wall clock.

"So, how'd he do it?" I asked everyone, including Sherm Campbell, the principal, Jake Catado, the assistant principal, and Harry Axhelm, the school's PE specialist. The most improbable event had occurred in front of my eyes and nothing had proceeded logically. No one booed, complained, or got up and left. In fact, no one said a word. Like Grandpa's unfortunate belch at dinner, everyone ignored the initial shock and the rest went on normally.

The best answer came from Sherm, who had retired from the Air Force at one of the very highest NCO ranks, command chief master sergeant. He shook his head, raised his eyebrows, and carefully explained that two things might account for the acceptance of Bill's joke. First, as the school's leader, Sherm's former rank was known and highly respected by air force personnel. The second, and more important, was that Bill Paterick was shot down in Europe piloting a B-24 during WW ll and was captured, becoming a POW for two years. Many of our parents knew it. The school's credibility with rank and file airmen was rock solid.

Bill grew up in Altoona, Pennsylvania, in a coal and steel region. He had the twang of a West Virginia accent. Many of his clothes came from garage sales. His hair was cut in a flat top and he was tall and thin with wide shoulders. At 16, he was working in the steel mills. He enlisted in the Air Force at 19 and piloted a bomber at 20 that was shot out of the air over Romania. His grandfather came to America as an indentured servant and worked without pay for seven long years before gaining his freedom.

During recesses, before and after school, Bill could be found in the Teachers' Lounge smoking cigarettes and gabbing. He told staff and students exciting stories of working in steel mills and being a POW. He told of eating rats and mice while being held captive and of watching a fellow worker at a mill fall into a boiling vat of steel and shrink up to the size of a small child because of the intense heat. In fact, he was a born story teller and the staff and kids loved it.

I learned a lot from Bill that I used in similar meetings with parents, like telling a joke or self-deprecating story to relax those in attendance. I learned that it is important to go out and meet people attending events and talk to them one on one and to personally get to know them. People with credibility are accorded more space than one might believe possible. Oh, and Bill did tell those assembled that he did not joke around about the topic or curriculum with students. Some parents that evening may have shaken their heads or frowned at Bill's inappropriate joke, but in the end, they trusted him to do the right thing. He wasn't viewed as an outsider or someone talking at them. Bill was considered down to earth and a proven leader, which means a lot in a mobile society like ours.

Chapter 28

THE SNOW DAY

Early in my teaching career, I found that effective teachers shape classes into distinctive personalities with strong bonds. "Okay. We're going to march down the hallway in single file. Do not look sideways to the right or left." I was in my third year of teaching in January of 1976 and had not yet gained tenure. It was important that we got this right because we were on a mission, and it had to be kept secret. The students walked as directed. The doors on both sides of the hallway were often left open for ventilation, and movement down the hall routinely drew attention from teachers or students, even if it was only one or two sets of eyes. It only took one or two glances by bored or distracted kids in classrooms to alert the rest of their class to anything out of the ordinary. In the current vernacular, we would be busted.

I was teaching a fifth-grade class at Center School on Travis Air Force Base. I grew up 20 miles away and was familiar with the weather patterns. What we were experiencing was something that occurred approximately every 25 years: significant snowfall in a climate that routinely averages 265 days of sunshine a year. During the night we had received over a foot and half of snow in many parts of the valley. The white fluffy snow piling up outside created an electric classroom environment. To add to the excitement, we saw occasional light flurries of white flakes slowly falling during the early morning hours of school. Students were amped up so introducing challenging material in reading, math, and science was a non-starter.

In most states, this small amount of snowfall meant very little. In our part of the Great Central Valley of California, it assumed the position of the elephant in the room, or should I say, playground. Classes had indoor recess and students were prohibited from playing outside. "Mr. Rott, why can't we play outside? Please let us play outside in the snow. We'll be good." Students peppered me with desperate pleas to engage the white form beckoning from outside. I knew that we weren't going to get much done on this particular day. Then one of the students threw out a challenge. "Mr. Rott, wouldn't it be great to write about our snow adventures in a writing assignment? We can make it out of the building without being caught and get ideas for stories."

Soon after starting my teaching career, I recognized that the proverbial "teaching moment" actually existed. I also discovered that students responded well to humor and the unexpected. As an example, in my first year, I found that students easily read a book turned upside down. I believe that a student, showing off, demonstrated how easy it was. I introduced it to the whole class. Even readers who were reading below average could do it. My classes learned how to read upside down every year from that time on. We did it for fun and practiced for the right occasion.

In a short time, a light went on somewhere deep and I threw out an idea to the class. "If anyone comes into our classroom wearing a tie or a suit looking important, slowly flip your book upside down and don't smile or look different in any way," I carefully instructed. We practiced a few times and the students loved it. Sure enough, within weeks, my principal and the district superintendent visited our classroom for an unscheduled observation. It worked. The faces the administrators made were priceless. When they left the classroom, students were ecstatic. The experience was unique to our class and a bond between us tightened. The administrators never said a word, which raised a lot of questions for which I have no answers.

I learned a valuable lesson. Students as a group came together each time we did something bizarre or different. A form of camaraderie developed and gave us an identity. Since that time, I have read accounts of people, especially in the armed services, who say that their units came together and became stronger after experiencing an unusual challenge in training or combat. It happens with young people in a school setting also.

We walked out into the snow without raising alarm and plodded carefully to part of the playground called the "upper deck," which was hidden from the rest of the school. Students had snowball fights, built snowmen, and generally frolicked in the snow until lunch. Then the class walked back inside the school and classroom pretending that we had just gone outside to use the restroom to wash up for lunch. As far as I know, our escapade went undetected. After the lunch break, we sat down with one more experience in common. The written stories on the snow theme were terrific, and the day became more productive than I ever thought possible.

Chapter 29

THE LIVE SAVING SQUEEZE

I can't remember much as we started dinner except that the ambient noise was extremely loud and everyone seemed to be laughing, talking, and eating at the same time. Suddenly the face across from me, my school colleague, Harry Axhelm, froze and turned red. He grabbed his neck, shook his head, and looked down. Something was wrong. I jumped up and ran around the table and grabbed him from behind and squeezed. An object like a dirt clod flew out of his mouth. I had performed the Heimlich Maneuver and it worked!

In 1975 I was approached about coaching the high school girls' junior varsity basketball team. I had no coaching experience but I had played basketball in high school and in city leagues in the area. The district coaching establishment thought that I was a perfect candidate as the Title 9 program still didn't produce enough women who were interested or qualified to coach at the high school level. I agreed and moved into a year of coaching a nice group of girls. They began calling me the "White Shadow" after a TV program of the day staring Ken Howard as a retired white NBA player who agrees to coach an inner-city team of girls who are all African-American. Our record was not impressive and after a mediocre year, I decided not to continue but to concentrate on my elementary teaching career and work on my Master's degree. My last obligation as a coach was to attend the annual coach's dinner. What a night that turned out to be.

The dinner would be held in Dixon at the Cattlemen's Steak House near my home, and I wouldn't have to drive to Fairfield or

Vacaville. I had never been to a coaches' dinner before and wasn't too sure what to expect. It sounded like it was going to get rowdy.

The dinner was an end-of-the-year social event that started out with cocktails and exchanging stories and jokes. Being new to the event and only 26, I was somewhat taken back by the wild nature of the activities flaming up in the steakhouse banquet room. I had never seen teachers behaving like sailors on a short leave.

"Have another, Rott."

"Let me buy you a drink, kid."

This went on for about 45 minutes. Finally, we were told to sit down and enjoy the wine as the steak dinners were served.

After the excitement with Harry's choking on a piece of his steak, we went back to our dinners. On my left sat one of the few women coaches. Marge Hoeft taught PE and science at the high school. She fit in well and told wild stories to the equal of any man present, and she was funny. Suddenly I noticed that she stopped participating in the conversations in her vicinity. She coughed and her head bent down. Her eyes became big and she shook her head. Before I knew what was happening, I was behind her, squeezing from behind in a bear hug. I noticed something dribbling out onto her lap. Some coaches yelled; others seemed transfixed as if they couldn't believe what they had just seen. I felt numb.

Later people from all over clapped me on the back and shook my hand. The manager of the restaurant thanked me. Everything was a blur of alcohol and excitement. "Great job, young man. Where did you learn that?" Where indeed? Sometime in the past I had a short introduction to the Heimlich during first aide training, I guessed.

For about a week after the dinner, teachers, custodians, and office staff called me a hero. Folks complimented me for acting so quickly twice during the coach's dinner. What are the odds? "Put your money away," people would say as I entered the Torch, a local bar hangout for teachers on Friday afternoons. For a short time, I became a celebrity.

Eventually, things died down and the only exciting thing happening to me occurred as I played basketball with my students on the playground when someone screamed, "Dunk it, Mr. Rott." But more exciting events were on the way.

Chapter 30

THE POISONOUS SMELL

The smell began as a mystery, a hint of what was yet to come, an unpleasant but distant scent that wasn't normal to a school that prided itself on cleanliness. As the workday continued, the odor grew. It didn't disappear as sometimes happened when the night custodian applied a new cleaning product to the floor or the student desks. At recess, teachers complained of headaches with a few describing dizziness or general discomfort.

Center School sat at the inside edge of Travis Air Force Base near the fenced area considered the "base" by those of us who worked there in the mid-70s. The school was twenty years old and was a sturdy, well-constructed and well-maintained facility. At night, all floors were mopped and polished for the start of a new day, a rather rare indulgence for a California public school, but possible for a school district receiving both state and federal funding.

"Dan, we need to get Jake and find out what that horrible smell is." Jan Rexroat was a second-grade teacher so she taught in the primary wing of the school. "I can't teach with this smell. What is it?'

"I don't know." I wasn't as distracted in my classroom but had noticed that something unfamiliar smelled throughout the school. At 27, I had been elected president of the Travis Unified Teachers Association. There was no collective bargaining, but staff were represented by employee associations. I was young, unmarried, had a BA in Political Science and had foolishly raised my hand to ask a question at an association meeting a year earlier. That's all it took. Older district teachers visited me to encourage and flatter me into agreeing to run for president. So as the association representative, I had to do something.

I sprinted through the hallways to the office to find Jake Catado, our principal. "Jake, what's that smell?"

Jake Catado was young for a principal. He had a gentle manner, and was totally committed to his job, the school and staff. He arrived early, left late and was willing to do whatever was necessary to make the school run smoothly.

"I think it might be the treatment for termites made last night around the school. The pest control company drilled holes and treated with chlordane. (Chlordane is a toxic pesticide that was banned in the United States in 1988 as harmful to humans and the environment. During the 70's a debate raged about whether it was safe.) The holes were sealed up and therefore contained. The smell shouldn't linger long."

Jake was wrong. The smell became stronger as the day progressed. At the end of the day, more teachers complained of headaches and some reported that they were nauseous. Teachers congregated in the staff room. As Jake entered, loud complaints and worried faces greeted his arrival. I too had been accosted and was the recipient of several notes from staff delivered by students during the course of the day. They all said the same thing. Something is wrong, and we need to find out what is going on.

An impromptu meeting was held, and Jake was peppered by upset and angry teachers. "Jake, I'm sick. Can't you do something? The smell is getting worse. What did the district office say?"

"The district is getting a representative of the pest control company to come out and work with our maintenance department to find out why this is happening," he solemnly reported.

I knew Jake was rattled. When he felt stress, his left eye lid fluttered uncontrollably. "Mr. Gammon says we will have a special staff meeting here tomorrow morning at 7:30 to report the results." Jake's eyelid was moving non-stop.

Mr. Gammon was the superintendent and considered the Father of the District since he was the only superintendent the district ever had.

The next morning as I arrived, I knew something big was happening. There were cars belonging to district office administrators including the business manager, several district maintenance trucks and at least three trucks with the bright red logo of the pest control company in front of the school.

What the hell is going on? I thought as I parked my car.

"Thank you for coming early for this special meeting." Mr. Gammon smiled his famous Grandpa smile. No one smiled back, even the administrators and pest company executives standing behind him. "Our crews came in last night and worked hard to find the cause of your complaints…blah, blah, blah. Unknown to us, pipes under the floors and part of the heating system punctured. Chlordane was inadvertently deposited into the vents, which circulated throughout the school and was delivered into classrooms."

"Excuse me, Mr. Gammon," said Jo Annala, the school's reading teacher and sharp as a piece of broken glass. "When you say *deposited*, do you mean pumped?"

"Well, that is a loaded word, but yes, in a manner of speaking."

The meeting dropped off a cliff at that point with staff loudly complaining. It got worse when a pest company foreman reported that there was no reason to worry. "I drank a water glass full of chlordane with no ill effects. We are recommending no treatment as the liquid evaporates naturally. There should be no harm to anyone except for the odor, which will quickly disappear."

I was on the phone to our association director at recess and was told I must call California Occupational Safety and Health Administration (CalOSHA). "Don't worry," said Ben, our association staff member. "It is completely confidential, and they will get results."

I was young but I was also scared to make that call. I liked my job. Would I be fired if word reached Mr. Gammon? I might never get another job and this was a great teaching position.

CalOSHA arrived the next day and ordered vents cleaned of all chlordane. The district apologized profusely to everyone. I kept my call confidential. Rumors spread that the district and the pest control company were being fined. At lunch the next day, I was told I had a call.

"Hello, Dan. This is Mr. Gammon. You know how much this district means to me."

"Yes sir," I stammered.

"I just got off the phone with the local CalOSHA director. He and I go back a long way. We were fraternity brothers at UC Berkeley. Do you know who made a call to CalOSHA? I want to speak with them. Did you make that call and a formal complaint, Dan?"

Oh, man... Someone once said, "Never lie, but if you do, make sure it is absolutely necessary."

I taught another twelve years in the Travis schools and was a principal for another 21 in a neighboring district. I discovered that sometimes you need to swallow your fear and do what you think is right. Sometimes it works.

Chapter 31

THE TEAM HONOR

There's nothing like the clink of a heavy prison gate to sharpen the senses. The noise is clear and metallic and vibrates in a way common to hallways made of concrete. There is no doubt that the object making the noise is heavy and formidable. By their nature, most prisons are full of hundreds of huge black and green painted metal doors. Almost every door shows scratches that are impossible to ignore.

My colleague, Don Moore, pointed this out as we entered what must have been our tenth door. "I can't understand how the doors get scratched. Who is free enough in here to have an object that scratches painted metal-bar gates?"

"I don't want to know," Ron Carr grimaced.

I carried my travel bag, as did the rest of my group, through door after door. The noise of the metal clicking and clanking, as a large metal key turns and opens the locks, is something that a short- term visitor will never forget. At 7:00 pm, our escort and the ten members of the team were the only people walking the long hallways. We passed several men wet-mopping the shiny concrete floors. Constant ambient noise rumbled and echoed throughout our walk. In some ways, I was reminded of the anonymous sounds heard in dog pounds, but instead of yapping and dog noises, men's voices, laughs, and whistles pierced the air at an uneven beat.

We were led into a changing room and heard the loud hollow sounds of basketballs hitting a wooden floor. Everything in the place seemed louder and with an ever-present echo. Jim Ochs, our team captain, blurted out, "Let's get dressed and hit the floor so we get in as many practice shots as possible. The last time I played here, we had trouble with depth perception because of the lighting."

In 1974, I was a member of the Straw Hat Pizza basketball team of the Vacaville Recreation League. We were in the top A league and won the championship easily. The honor of playing at the Vacaville State Prison was ours, and I didn't know what to expect. One of my roommates for a year at Chico State, Steve Ceriani was also on our fast city league team. I wasn't as good as most of the members of the team, but the more I played with them in A League, the better I became.

Steve yelled on the way out to the court, "Come on, you guys. You're not afraid, are you? Haaaa." Most guys quietly "dressed out," not Steve. He had a goofy, hyper personality. The rest of us quietly dressed and jogged out into the prison gym.

"Wow. This is really something," whispered Tom Newsom, whom we called Neus, when we tracked down the same ball during free shoot around. He'd grown up in Vacaville and played linebacker and defensive end for Boise State for a couple of years before dropping out and coming back to work and live in his hometown. He was one of those guys whose neck was eclipsed by his thick back and shoulder muscles. He had the biggest block head I'd ever seen. We positioned him under our basket and let him grab rebounds. He sometimes shot when we had the ball, but usually he passed after grabbing a rebound to one of our top shooters like Jim or Steve.

"Man, you're not kidding," I responded, as "Neus" admired the facility. The basketball court was shaped like a large wooden bowl with elevated bench seats like those in old high school or small college gyms. "Room for 500." I estimated that half of the seats were taken when we "hit the floor," and by the time the game started, the place was full.

The crowd was a diverse mix of white, black, and Hispanic men yelling and whistling. Johnny Cash at Folsom Prison flashed through my mind. I couldn't help notice that some of the men wore lipstick and sat with their arms around other men. I must admit that in

1974, this was quite a shock. I hadn't expected to see men in makeup and cuddling in a full lock-down prison garb. Everyone appeared to be in a good mood though and ready to watch basketball.

I really can't remember who won the game, but I do remember the prison team played well and were good sports. In fact, they were probably the nicest team we played all year. "Shoot the ball, skinny" was the meanest thing I heard that night.

After the game, we showered and were taken to a snack bar opened for our benefit. We ordered hamburgers, fries, sodas, and milkshakes. Prisoners cooked and waited on us.

"I wouldn't mind coming back here next year. They played good basketball," remarked Don as we headed out to our cars. Don was the best all-around player on the team. His time as a college player gave him special credibility with the guys. The event impressed him, and that was all I needed, and I agreed.

"That was fun. I didn't think I'd like it. Let's work hard to come back," I announced boldly.

We didn't go back. That was the only time I visited the prison. Life goes on and events change. I can't remember why we didn't return, but it might very well be that prison policy changed, and the life in prisons became more dangerous. Gangs and the mentally ill became more prevalent. The Anti-Drug Act signed by President Reagan and Clinton's Violent Crime Control Act directed harsher penalties and longer times in prison for offenders. Public policy toward convicts became harsher and prison populations grew rapidly. Mental hospitals closed nationwide. Attitudes hardened on all sides. Research shows that more prisons had little long-term effect on the levels of crime in most communities. At the same time, prisons became more dangerous.

Chapter 32

THE WORST PROPOSAL EVER

The single most important event in my life occurred in 1977 on a beautiful fall day in Sacramento. I drove nervously into the short driveway and started thinking about my decision to propose. I was in a sweet spot in my life with a steady salary and job security, and I felt I had achieved a certain amount of success as a teacher.

I had met someone who instantly attracted me. When I first saw Joan, she stood taller than most of the girls in the room. I noticed her dark hair and blue-green eyes. She was standing at the stair railing listening to the band at D. O. Mills, a popular dance spot in Old Sacramento. I thought she was the most beautiful girl in the building, and I half-expected that she would say no when I approached her or that she was with the band. "Hi, do you want to dance?" I shouted over the noise.

She smiled and said, "Sure." We danced and spoke for about an hour before the band quit for the night.

We exchanged phone numbers and I called her the next week and arranged for the first of many dates. We went to movies, had special dinners, and excursions to the beach and the mountains. She practiced cooking Japanese food for me that she was learning in a multicultural class at Sacramento State.

After we parked, my mind came back to the present. I jumped out and the warm fall sun made the occasion feel even more radiant. The anticipation of what I was about to do charged through my body. My mind refocused on the task at hand. I ran around and held her door open. We held hands as we walked to the white building with the red door. I made sure we sat in a seat at the far end of the room. After getting us a drink, I pretended to relax as I looked at her and tried to smile casually. I only hoped I wouldn't stutter and trip over my words. To say I knew very little about these things was an understatement. I read only historical fiction, liked action movies, my sister was unmarried, and my parents were first-generation immigrants, who like their parents, didn't talk much about personal issues.

Finally, I calmed myself enough to ask, "Joan, I love you and want to live with you for the rest of my life. Will you marry me?" I tried to smile confidently, but something in her face didn't look right. I waited.

She looked at me for the longest time. She finally shook her head slightly, looked me directly in the eye, and answered. "No."

I felt like crawling under the table. Feebly I responded, "You won't?"

"No." she answered simply. "I won't accept a proposal of marriage in a Dairy Queen."

The next weekend, I proposed properly at the best restaurant I could find, one located in the hills near Folsom. We were married for 40 years, had three children, and four grandchildren. We laughed many times as we recalled the time Dan proposed. During our marriage when we went out for dinner or special events, I always told her she was the most beautiful lady in the room and I was glad I proposed, even if it happened twice.

Chapter 33

THE LUNG COLLAPSE

"This is not going to be your best night," the young doctor remarked as we looked at an x-ray taken an hour earlier. "You're going to need to stay here tonight for sure and we'll see what happens after that."

He looked like ER doctors I had seen a few times on TV. Casual with a white coat covering a collared shirt open at the top, Levis, and a well-worn but expensive pair of sneakers. Without the white coat, he looked like so many young men who crowd together at upscale bars at happy hour to watch the latest sports game or meet close friends after work.

I had come to the ER a couple of hours earlier with my closest friend after my wife insisted I get checked. For the past two days I had been complaining about an odd feeling I had in my left side. There were no sharp pains but a feeling of pressure caused me to believe that I had pulled a muscle or had slept on my side the wrong way. I started to feel shortness of breath, but at 34 I was still playing city league basketball and being short of breath was not a strange sensation. Joan, called one of my best friends and a former roommate at Chico State, Larry "Dyke" Dykstra, and asked him to take me to our hospital's ER in Sacramento. She decided to stay home with the kids but was adamant that I not drive myself.

The waiting room was crowded, uncomfortable, and unpleasant. People coughed, sneezed, and wiped noses onto shirt sleeves and what looked like napkins pilfered at the local McDonalds. A small girl sat with her mother at the end of the room with what looked like a broken or badly twisted arm. She sobbed softly and her mother rubbed her back and whispered encouragement. At least twice, I looked over at Dyke and said things like, "Everyone in here is sick or look like hell. Let's get out of here."

I had met Larry Dykstra at Chico State. We were Political Science majors who thought we were destined to teach high school history or civics someday. We started teaching elementary school with double credentials allowing us to teach any level K-12. Transferring to high school was just a matter of time as social science positions were rarely available. We both enjoyed elementary school and stayed in our careers working with younger students.

Dyke maintained a *don't go there* look on his face as I nagged to leave. Finally, he shook his head as he said, "No. Joan thinks it's important and she'd kill me if I took you home before seeing a doctor. I'm sure they'll call your name soon." I wanted to go home. I also wanted to get away from people who were obviously sick, hurting or making odd noises, but I waited uncomfortably until my name was called.

Eventually I was led to a waiting area to get a routine exam: stethoscope, body thumping and general observation. A technician walked me to an x-ray machine. "Raise your left arm, look forward and try not to breathe," he instructed professionally as I rolled my eyes.

After being escorted back to the waiting room, I was more anxious than ever to leave. "I'm sure I passed the tests. No one said a word about anything. This is embarrassing. Let's get out of here. I have papers to correct. I'm sure they'll call if it's something important." Nothing worked on Dyke. We stayed.

Then out of the corner of my I eye I saw the doctor who did my initial exam walking back to where Dyke and I were sitting. "Mr. Rott, please follow me."

I gave Dyke that *oh, oh* look and got up. I mumbled something like, "This doesn't look good," and laughed nervously. The doctor smiled politely.

In his office, we began the examination of the x-ray, backlit for easy viewing. He mentioned this not being my "best night" and that I had suffered a collapsed lung. He continued by saying it was not an ordinary collapsed lung. As the left lung collapsed, a large amount of fluid had filled my chest cavity and was pushing my heart creating a dangerous condition that needed to be addressed immediately before I had an unspecified *cardiac event*. Unlike my wife, who would have grilled the doctor, I didn't ask questions and trusted that the doctor knew what needed to be done.

I returned to the waiting room, told Dyke I had to stay due to a collapsed lung, called Joan and explained what had happened, and returned to a unit in the emergency room with a bed surrounded by drab hospital curtains. I was quickly prepped and a tube was inserted into my chest to relieve pressure and remove the fluid that had settled in my pulmonary cavity. Little did I know that this was the first of five tubes that would be pushed into my chest. The first incision felt like I had been stabbed through my rib cage and occurred within minutes of saying, "You might feel a sting." The other insertions in the next two weeks were either not as painful or I got used to the sting.

The ER doctor I spoke to that first night was only partly correct. In most cases, the lung re-inflates and the patient is sent home the next day, but conventional treatment didn't work in my case. I stayed at the hospital for almost three weeks and they were not my best days or nights. Eventually, a surgeon removed part of my left lung and I started to think of myself as a human pincushion with tubes pushed into and out of my chest. Finally, after three weeks, I went home to rehab and regain the strength to go back to work. This incident was quite a shock and affected me in many ways for months after. Psychologically I carried the emotional scars of feeling vulnerable and uncertain about my health and attitude toward life. My carefree sense of personal freedom shifted. I promised to no longer take my best days and nights for granted.

Chapter 34

THE PARACHUTE RIDE

"Oh, my god. Dan, it's a thunder shower and it's coming our way," Joan said anxiously. We stood on a Northwest pier searching the huge expanse of Lake Tahoe trying to locate our children. Normally the weather in the Tahoe basin is warm and inviting during August, but wind and short thunderstorms can develop without warning. As we watched, huge dark clouds began growing and changed from slate to gun barrel gray. "What about the kids? Are they safe out there?"

Earlier in the day, we had left our cabin at the top of Donner Summit and driven to a new adventure. We had seen an ad in one of the local tourist papers found in most retail stores, which advertise places to enjoy nearby. Each year we found something new and exciting.

On returning from the Serene Lakes store, I found Joan in the bedroom. "It looks like they have parachute rides in King's Beach. Two can ride at a time. Ivan and Tara might like it. I'm getting tired of walking around the lakes."

After a beautiful ride down the summit to the highway that snakes along the Truckee River, we turned north at the lake from Tahoe City to Kings Beach. We saw two boats towing parachutes moving quickly away into what is called the most beautiful lake in the world. The passengers' legs dangled and moved playfully until they were gone. We parked the van and everyone jumped out.

A large sign announcing "Parasailing Rides" sat next to a modest wooden kiosk. Inside, leaning out the top window portion of a Dutch door was a young man with bleached blond hair and skin tanned the color of a football. His nose was covered with white zinc oxide lotion to protect his nose from sunburn like thousands of young men and women found on beaches around the world, especially California. I'd often thought that the only way to get a job on a beach was to match this look.

Tara, 11, and Ivan, 8, smiled and laughed as they charged toward the pier. Our children were shy and a bit reserved, but not this day. Excitement radiated from them as they moved to the kiosk to sign up. "There's no way they'll get up in those things," I shared quietly with Joan as we walked down the boat ramp. I was wrong.

The speedboat leaped and slid forward to the middle of the lake. The harnesses strapped both kids into their seats tightly. They sat firmly buckled in. A metal tow line connected the parachute and seat assembly to a huge spool slowly unwinding as the boat gained speed. The parachute rose high above the lake and I had to wonder, *Have we made a big mistake here? I didn't think they would do this for all the pizza in Lake Tahoe.*

A pleasant summer breeze blew toward us as we stood on the pier watching the colorful red, white and blue parachute disappear over the horizon. But in the time it took to tie a shoe, the wind picked up and the lightly colored clouds changed to something darker and more threatening. Swells grew into breakers. Then we saw a flash. Within seconds there was a loud crack and then a boom.

We raced over to the kiosk. The young man was speaking on a round hand-held walkie talkie favored by police departments at that time. "There's nothing to worry about. The boat is making a turn and coming back to the pier."

"But what about the thunder and lightning?" Joan responded with irritation.

"Distances are hard to judge in the lake. Don't worry. The drivers are experienced and know what they're doing," he tried to explain. I masked my alarm.

Soon we saw a speck coming our way from far out on the lake. The sun went behind the clouds and the day became darker. The mountain bowl surrounding the lake changed to darker colors.

"I guess this wasn't a good idea," I told Joan and then immediately regretted my words. In the next instant, huge mountain rain drops fell and my shoulders were wet and cold. And then it started to hail.

After what seemed like hours, the parachute and our kids came in to view. The tow boat crashed up and down through the wind-swept waves. Dark storm clouds with thunder followed the boat like a huge black bear lumbering after small mountain prey. The weather went through at least three cycles of sun and warmth back to darkness and heavy cloud cover. The rain and hail stopped and started several times. Crashing thunder and lightning remained a constant backdrop to the drama playing out on the beach as we watched and agonized over the safety of our kids.

The most improbable ending occurred when the boat and parachute reached the pier near the beach where we stood transfixed with fear. As the wench pulled the kids out of the sky, we saw that they wore their best Disneyland smiles. What a relief! After we reunited and the adventure was recounted by both groups, we headed to lunch and a happy reunion eating pizza at Boatside Pizza. I knew that I needed to be a little more careful when I picked a new family outing, but I've always thought that a life worth living is a life with excitement, adventure, and a brush with risk. Our summer excursions at Donner Summit tested the wisdom of that philosophy.

Chapter 35

THE TRAIL RIDE

"Are you Mr. Rott?

A young man about 20 old had slowly coasted a pickup into the driveway of our cabin property in Serene Lakes at Donner Summit and got out. My oldest son, Erik, and I were restacking wood next to the A-Frame. Summer chores are a regular part of owning property in the mountains and July of 1994 worked well with my schedule to do just that.

"What can I do for you?" I asked, puzzled by the serious look on his face.

"I've been told to come and tell you that your wife has been hurt and is at Donner Summit Ski Ranch. She was in an accident. Someone needs to come and get the kids who are with her."

"What happened? How bad is it?" I stammered.

Earlier in the day, Joan had taken Tara and Ivan to the ski resort to go on a horse trail ride. She had reserved three horses and a guide for a short ride near the ski facility. During the summer months, ski resorts often find ways to bring tourists back to ride horses, bikes, or motorized mini-cars that are driven around the huge parking lots, *grand-prix* fashion.

"Is she okay?" My voice grew louder. I was starting to panic but realized that my Erik, 13, was standing next to me, and I needed to dial the concern level down a notch.

"I'm sorry. That's all I know for sure. Please follow me."

My wife has the van. I don't have transportation. We need to go with you."

He walked quickly to the truck and said curtly, "Get in."

My anxiety level spiked.

I don't remember the ride to the Donner ski area. As soon as we reached the parking lot, we saw an emergency vehicle and EMT personnel talking and gesturing. Two men dressed in EMT blue fatigues with yellow suspenders were in the back of the ambulance working on someone lying on a gurney. Others were talking to a Sheriff's Deputy at his truck, which was parked nearby. I still didn't know how serious the situation was for Joan.

Tara and Ivan ran towards Erik and me. As I watched them come, out of the corner of my eye I noticed feet in blood-soaked socks hanging over the back end of the gurney. One foot twisted sideways, sending a shock through my body. I heard a muffled moan and then another.

As I approached the ambulance, an EMT member, told me to back up and move away from the emergency vehicle. "We're getting ready to transport," he said matter of factly.

"Where?" is all I could blurt out.

"Tahoe Forest Hospital." They closed the doors and pulled away with the red emergency lights flashing.

I drove the van and the three kids to the hospital. Tara told me that on the way down the hill, the guide had been bucked and thrown from his horse when they encountered the loud *whoosh* of a large water sprinkler, which sounds much the same as a large rattlesnake. The horses spooked. (A water system is used to keep vegetation on ski runs alive in summer months to anchor snow during ski season.) Joan's horse jolted forward and followed the guide's horse to the cobblestone parking lot, where she was thrown onto her ankles, shattering one while a horse hoof crushed the other. The guide jumped up immediately and grabbed the reins of the two horses carrying the kids. At ages 13 and 10, this was their first trail ride.

As we waited in a room adjacent to the emergency room, a young doctor walked in and asked to speak with me. Joan had indeed broken both ankles, although a better word "is shattered," he confided. He let me speak with Joan, who was heavily sedated and probably in shock. I kissed her and whispered the kids were fine.

About this time, I heard two doctors talking in the next room as the doors were open. "Wow! Skip, take a look at this x-ray when you get a chance. Don't see many like that."

Soon a doctor called me aside and said, "Your wife will receive the best care possible. I'll explain later. Now I want you to know we need to get busy and adjust her ankles."

"Oh, sure. Okay. I appreciate the updates."

"AAAHHHHHHHHH!" The kids and I were jerked alert by one of the loudest screams I had ever heard. I asked a passing nurse what the noise was and she said that a patient had her ankles "adjusted." Evidently, I didn't understand a medical term for manually straightening broken bones. The doctor thoughtfully disclosed the procedure to prepare us. It didn't work. Memories of my own painful experience, a simple wrist break in high school, flooded my head.

Joan's parents drove up the same day and took the kids home with them to Sacramento. Joan stayed at the Truckee hospital for four days and I slept at the cabin.

During her stay, doctors told us we were lucky. One of the finest orthopedic surgeons on the West Coast performed surgery and repaired her damaged ankles. Interestingly enough, he was there on call, as he had been selected by the Secret Service to be called if the President of the United States needed emergency treatment on the West Coast. At the time, doctors were on call at different locations throughout the nation for that purpose depending on their specialty and need.

Taking an ambulance home was deemed prohibitively expensive. Hospital personnel carried and placed her in our van. I was instructed to call the Dixon Fire Department when I got home for assistance with getting her into the house. Once home, a large fire truck was there, and four burly firemen lifted her and put her on a hospital bed neighbors had set up in our living room. Joan slept and lived there for six months.

During her rehabilitation, I became a believer in handicapped accommodations and gained insight into the challenges of our wheelchair-bound population. Over the years, Joan had at least three more major surgeries to stabilize her ankles, allowing her to walk pain-free without a limp. We hiked all over the world. I was amazed at, and admired, her courage and spirit.

Chapter 36

THE CONFERENCE FROM HELL

"I need to talk to you," said Bub. His voice was low and even like a car ferry plying ocean waters across the bay: confident and determined. Earlier in the day, I had a message that Gerald "Big Bub" McIntyre wanted a meeting with me. It was a Friday in 1989 and I was in my second year as principal of Anderson School. Resolving complaints from parents was an important part of the job. Sight unseen, this promised to be a doozey.*

Growing up, I had heard about the McIntyres being rough people but I'd lived in Chico and Vacaville for at least ten years and I didn't remember Bub as he was six years younger than me. Today's conference promised to be a difficult one as a staff member had filed a serious Child Protective Services complaint alleging that Bub's fourth-grade daughter had been injured the night before at the family home. A dangerous knife game between Bub and his dad with the girl as a prop resulted in a small but significant cut on her finger. Although CPS complaints filed were legally confidential, parents generally blamed the school and more specifically, the teacher, for "turning them in." Most accused parents felt a need to vent, complain, or profess their innocence. The accepted protocol was to maintain a curtain of confidentiality and refuse to engage anyone on the matter. All formal complaints were investigated, and all corrective actions were solely the responsibility of CPS. We had no choice, however, but to listen. I needed to draw the angry parent away from the teachers and provide a forum for school and parent interaction.

I'm a big man, but no one told me about Bub. I tried not to stare. He weighed at least 250 pounds and stood close to six feet tall. His shiny, shaved bald head resembled the custom yellow bowling ball I had once seen at the Lodi Bowling Lanes when I was a kid. A silver earring in the shape of a lightning bolt hung from one ear and moved slightly as he walked. He wore a white t-shirt and denim bib overalls with black military style boots. In many ways, he resembled the iconic wrestler of the late 1960s who went by the name of Haystack Calhoun.

I escorted him into the conference room between my office and the school office. The round table was, like much of the school's furniture, old and well worn. I might have been uncomfortable but I didn't feel particularly nervous. I was aware that conferences with angry parents moved quickly to a difficult level in the blink of an eye, but I found that being a local helped my credibility at school and in the community. At least it did in most cases.

"So, you're Mr. Rott," Bub sneered. His voice remained level and controlled.

I nodded my head and said, "I am." I hoped my tone was relaxed but authoritative.

Then he jumped to a topic I hadn't expected. "Your dad was my principal." He paused for effect. I wasn't sure what was coming next. He leaned slightly forward and said in a quiet but forceful voice, "He spanked me and I didn't like it."

At that point I must have lost all sense of perspective. "Well, we don't do that any longer. Against state law." As if that was the current issue or that it had anything to do with the conference. I don't think I had enough moisture in my mouth to smile, but I tried to look helpful.

"And now I'm meeting with you about a report to CPS about my daughter." His green eyes locked on me like a laser. "I'm not worried. It was an accident involving my dad. I just want you to know we aren't happy with the school turning us in."

I really can't remember much about the rest of the meeting except it was short and not adversarial. I do remember one more thing he said before he left. "You're sure a nervous guy."

I remember thinking, *Aw, man.*

Bub left as the bell rang ending the day for students. He didn't shake my hand but he did walk out calmly. That was the last time I saw him.

Two weeks later, I read the local paper, *The North County Reporter,* like I did every morning. One of the lead stories read "Couple Shot on County Road in Drug Bust Gone Bad." These were not my favorite stories so I skimmed the article until I got to the part where it said that, "Gerald McIntire was quickly arrested in the early morning hours as the shooter and is currently being held in the Solano County Jail."

"*Ah, man.....*" was about all I could mumble.

*Names and dates were changed here for confidentiality.

Chapter 37

THE SHOCKING CRASH

"The car hit the truck head on and in a matter of seconds they both blew up," my mother said solemnly. I dropped the phone and walked past my secretaries and down the steps leading to the street and my car. I was in shock and I felt numb as though I was sitting in a large bubble. The tears started soon after. Wednesday, March 2, 1994 proved to be a very long day.

On Monday, February 28, my family and I took the day off to take my Norwegian cousin and his family to the San Francisco airport. Kjell's grandmother, Elen Karine, and my Grandma Johnson were sisters. His wife Aud, and his daughters Linda and Suzanna had come to California during the Winter Olympics in Lillihammer. They lived in the smaller village of Hammer, a short distance from Lillihammer, and decided to leave the area for three weeks to escape the crowds and congestion forecast for the 1994 Olympic events.

"Good-by. I'll miss you." Tara said affectionately. Tara and Suzanna were about the same age and had bonded closely during the short time they had spent at our house. Tara helped Suzanna learn how to roller blade in the street in front. That was the current fad at the time. Suzann taught Tara how to play Edvard Grieg's famous "In the Hall of the Mountain King" on the family piano. It's sometimes called the "Silly Symphony," and I had heard it a time or two as background for a Disney movie. We all said our goodbyes and promised to see each other soon.

Although they visited California for three weeks, their stay with us lasted for less than a week. The rest of the time they traveled to as many places in California as possible. As a matter of fact, they are the only people I ever heard speak well of Motel 6. "It doesn't have to be fancy, just clean." Kjell informed us. Many Europeans are not fond of the new and pretentious.

He also did his research. "There is a 'Rent-a-Wreck' dealership in Davis. Can you take me there to get a car?" he asked. Kjell owned a car repair shop in Hammer and was comfortable with cars. He quickly rented a 12-year-old car at an incredibly low price although that wouldn't have worked for me.

The family called us several times as they crisscrossed Southern California taking in the sights. "We saw a Cadillac belonging to Marilyn Monroe," he announced excitedly in one conversation. Kjell restored cars at home and was an American car enthusiast. He showed me a photo of his beautifully restored Chrysler New Yorker St. Regis. I introduced him to a friend of mine in Dixon who had a 1957 red Corvette convertible. They took off and spent three hours cruising around Dixon, Winters, and Davis. I became concerned and started to worry. Finally they arrived and Kjeill announced, "That was worth the price of the trip."

Things had changed greatly since my grandmother left a poor area of Norway in the early 20th century. The standard of living had vastly improved and now people were mostly prosperous. Their schools were well run and students were taught several languages. Most Norwegians speak fluent English with an American accent. Suzanna understood English but did not speak much as she wasn't as fluent as the rest of her family. Kjell, Aud, and Linda spoke as well or better than we did. While Grandma Johnson lived for more than 85 years in Minnesota and yet retained a heavy Scandinavian accent. When we visited places with Kjell and his family, no one realized that they were from Europe.

"Let's go to the Hard Rock Café in Sacramento. They play lots of country western music," I offered on the Saturday before they were scheduled to go home. I never thought that Europeans adored Garth Brooks, but these Norwegians did. On that afternoon, Joan and I sat and nursed a beer as Kjell and Aud showed us how they deftly navigated Texas line dancing on the big dance floor. They offered several times to teach us but we'd tried previously and failed miserably. We all smiled and laughed at our "Cowboy Norwegian" cousins.

On Sunday, February 27, we slept in and prepared to have a comfortable day together before our guests went home. The Olympics were rolling to an end, Kjell needed to get back to work, and his girls anxiously wanted to get back to school.

"What time are Bea and Dian coming over for the BBQ?" asked Kjell. He had met my mother and sister while they were visiting Norway several years earlier.

"I think Mom said 1:00," I answered. "I'm washing my car. Want to help?"

Kjell and I washed my car as Suzanna and Linda played out in front shooting baskets and skating with our kids. Although it was February, the sun was out and we were having a typical 70° California day. Kjell and Aud loved our climate and couldn't believe that we had orange, palm, and redwood trees growing in our backyard.

We all felt so comfortable with each other. Later as we barbecued steaks, I remarked, "Life can't get any better than this." One of my favorite expressions at the time was "Is this a great country, or what?" What indeed.

A little over a week after I got the phone call from my mom, I received a letter from Aud, who described what had happened

" *We had been home for about three hours when Kjell and Suzanne went to pick up our dog. They loved her so they couldn't wait till the next day to see her. I couldn't stop them and I didn't really try to because I knew how much they were looking forward to seeing Nikita. On their way back home the theory is that Kjell fell asleep and therefore crashed into a big truck. They were killed at once so they didn't feel anything.*"

We were devastated. Tara was especially hit hard. She cried for two days. It's odd how our mind works after a traumatic event. For a year or so I marked time by counting the times I washed my car like I had with Kjell on that Sunday morning. I stopped counting after I got to 30. Ivan and his new wife Sammy, Joan, and I are planning a trip to Norway to visit Aud and Linda. We'll also pay our respects to Kjell and Suzanna.

Chapter 38

THE AGATE HUNTERS

"Dad, what are they doing?" Erik stood by my side while we waited for the rest of the family to catch up with us. Finally, everyone jumped off the last terraced step. The engineered switchback trail led us from the tall bluffs to the ocean beach below.

"What are they looking for, Dad?" Tara asked as we walked on the beach. Dozens of people were on their knees digging or sifting through sand. Others were walking bent over or stooping to pick up something that caught their eye. A few carried bags or containers with things we didn't recognize. I saw a man thrust something into his bulging front pocket. We started walking slowly on the large curved beach away from the crowds, but our curiosity grew.

When Joan joined us a few minutes later, she said, "They must be looking for shells." We kept moving down the beach closer to the large north coast waves with water cracking and pounding the beach into submission. The smell of ocean air washed over us as we ran to stay away from foamy, ocean tendrils pushing in our direction. We loved the coast and the activities that attracted each of us as we explored and played in our own way.

The summer fog was starting to break and the dark, gloomy skies opened up with translucent patches of alternating shades of gray as light shone through at odd angles. Earlier the drive from Prairie Creek State Park on Highway 101 had been slow and tense.

"I can't see a thing. Watch on your side," I reminded Joan. I squinted like I was reading the small print of an insurance form. A tourist magazine had highlighted Patrick's Point 44 miles south of where we were camping. We decided to travel and explore for the day. We didn't anticipate the difficulty of driving in the fog, but our luck was changing in many ways.

On the way back to the stairs to walk up from the beach in the late afternoon, I couldn't resist. "What are you looking for?" I asked a lady who carried a long stick while digging in the sand. Her other hand held a small canvas bag.

"Agates," she replied with a friendly smile.

"Agates? What are agates?"

She stopped and opened her bag and pulled out several white translucent stones. Each was rounded and displayed different shades of white and cream. A few were multicolored with alternating clear, milky white, and cream shading. No two were alike. I was reminded of the sky when the fog broke hours before.

"If you're really interested, go talk to John, from Texas," she advised. "He's the tall guy with waders, a long-handled scoop, and a large brimmed hat."

"John, from Texas?" I asked with what must have been a quizzical expression on my face.

"He knows everything about agate hunting." She looked over toward the sandy beach and the patches of rounded beach gravel where most of the people had congregated.

"Well, what do you think?" I asked the family, but my mind was made up. I was already heading toward John from Texas. Little did I know it but a 30-year relationship was about to begin.

John hunted passionately for agates every chance he got. He lived in San Antonio, Texas, with his wife, an elementary school teacher. He sharp features were visible under what looked like a fly fisherman's fedora. He wore a long-sleeved shirt and fishermen waders complete with angler suspenders. A long arm was grasping a 3-foot piece of PVC pipe that had a plastic perforated serving spoon pushed into the opening at the end. Duct tape completed the tool, fastening the spoon tightly to the hollow pipe. The scoop was used to snatch agates and colored rocks from the surf and sand.

John and his wife, who spent her time reading, camped at Patrick's Point for most of the summer. They would also pack their large camper style van and drive night and day during Christmas break to reach Patrick's Point to settle in for five days as John roamed the winter coast looking for the big ones that kicked up during big Pacific storms. The beach at the park is known as Agate Beach.

Using the best multitasking technique, I have ever encountered, John scoured the beach, picking up rocks with his handmade tool, examining them closely, while talking and answering our questions. Every few minutes, he would drop a rock into the clean plastic milk bottle tied to his waist with a short thin rope. "Why don't y'all poke around and I'll help you out, if you're interested," he kindly offered in a strong traditional Texas accent. He took a moment to pull several nice stones out of his reconditioned milk jug and let us carefully examine his prize agates of the day. We were as excited as if they were gold nuggets.

An hour or two sped by until it was time to go back to Prairie Creek. We all ran back to John to share our harvest of beautiful white rocks. John smiled and reported, "No, not this time. But agate hunting is like fishing. It takes time to get it right." Our plain white beach quartz were not agates. We vowed to come back. That winter, we went to the library and learned everything possible about agates. The next year, with John's mentoring, we developed "agate eyes" and could spot an agate 10 feet away. We've treasured our time at the beach hunting for at least three decades. John, now retired, lives in a small modular home near the park. We still gather as a family once a year for a few days with daughters-in-law and grandchildren as we continue hunting for the big ones and sew another thread as family.

Chapter 39

THE BEGINNING OF THE END

The paramedic jumped out of his truck at the same time I started walking up the steps of the modest duplex. My sister had purchased the south side of the building on this quiet street a block from the middle school about twenty years earlier after her short marriage fell apart. My mother stood on the walkway with one of her friends, Bev Fox.

"What happened, Mom?"

"Which way?" said the first of two firemen as they reached us.

"Straight in and then to the left," said Mom.

The two figures clad in dark blue walked briskly but without any indication of alarm.

Once again, I asked my mom, "What's going on?" I was afraid something serious had happened to my sister. "You've never called me from work before. Did something happen to Dian? Is she in trouble?"

"She was on the floor throwing up black stuff, so I got worried." Mom stated, her voice surprisingly even.

Before I pressed for the meaning of her reply, one of the firemen ran quickly out of the house and opened the back of the emergency vehicle. As he raced past us holding a pack, he turned and said, "Why didn't you tell us it was an emergency? We were told that someone had fallen out of bed."

Mom looked confused but calm at the same time. Bev Fox put her hand on Mom's shoulder and started rubbing it. Bev lived down the street and was a friend of both my mom and sister. I noticed a couple of years back that Dian socialized with my mom's friends almost exclusively and saw people her own age less and less.

Now I was becoming alarmed. "Did you call 911? What did you say, Mom?"

"She was on the floor," my mother said, as she looked away, but her answer still didn't make sense.

At some time in our conversation, a heavy-duty pick-up truck with Dixon Fire Department markings arrived, and two more blue-clad figures carrying large bags ran past us into the open door. I didn't see any faces, only the blur of blue-colored uniforms. As a town native and an elementary school principal, I knew many local first responders. Still I couldn't distinguish identities as they ran past us.

Two days before, Mom called and said she needed to go over and stay at Dian's house because my sister wasn't feeling well. She was concerned and needed to monitor my sister and to make sure she ate good food. I wasn't shocked or even surprised.

My sister was an alcoholic and retired from the University of California, Davis at the early age of 53. She had had a good job in the Provost's Office, and we were proud of her achievements. We didn't understand the nature of a closet drinker. She never went to bars or drank heavily in front of us. Eventually, the seriousness of her issues became known after a colleague called with concerns about problems at her work. After a painful confrontation and family intervention, Dian resigned her job and sought help with medical specialists.

Mom and I drove her to Vallejo for rehab sessions where she seemed to thrive and enjoy the program. On our drives back and forth, she was pleased with her progress but refused to discuss anything of a personal nature. Dian called me on one occasion to help her dispose of fancy gift bottles of alcoholic beverages and liqueurs. With our help, a rehabilitation stint and an Alcoholics Anonymous sponsor, we all felt optimistic concerning her attitude and our future as an extended family healing and moving forward.

I saw movement and the young man who had raced past us when I arrived walked slowly through the door taking off a pair of latex gloves. He addressed us together. "I'm sorry, but she's gone." Mom cried and I stood stunned. Now both Bev and I had our hands on my mom's shoulders. *How is it possible that my younger sister is gone?* I thought.

As I tried to process what occurred, I learned that my mom found hidden bottles of vodka in the house in her stay. She diligently poured out the contents, searched the house, and thought she had extinguished the threat it posed, only to realize that somewhere more bottles remained carefully hidden. Dian quietly located a secret spot and drank in the dark, deep into the night after Mom turned in to sleep. Early the next morning, Mom heard noises and found her sick on the floor and called 911. She told them, "Someone fell out of bed and needs help."

Later that day, Mom, Joan, and I met with two men at the Coroner's Office. After asking what happened that morning, one of the men looked Mom's way and asked, "Was your daughter sick or not feeling well?"

Mom hesitated, looked up, turned her head sideways, and answered, "No. No I don't think she was sick or anything."

My head whipped around. I looked at Joan and her face flashed a painful look. I quickly interjected with an exasperated voice, "Mom?" I then addressed the man in the suit. "My sister is an alcoholic and has been treated for her addiction and accompanying medical issues."

I then looked back at Mom. Her face showed no emotion. Her eyes were empty. I knew her response to the question was not a purposeful attempt to evade or mislead. A sense of nausea struck as I realized I didn't recognize the person sitting in front of me.

From then on, Mom had good days and bad days before I enrolled her in a locked memory/dementia facility in Vacaville. Within the year, her condition worsened. In a short time, she too was gone.

Chapter 40

THE HOUSE FIRE

"Get out! Get out now! There's a fire!"

I turned my gaze from the Giants game to see a young, dark-haired Hispanic woman in her early 20s standing in our house. Her face was contorted into a wild look and she gestured with her arm several times in rapid movements toward the garage.

Instead of moving my head rapidly in her direction, I turned slightly and stared. I tried to figure out the meaning of the interruption. I thought, *Why is an unknown woman yelling at me in my own home?* My quiet time in my favorite green leather recliner was being loudly violated. With three kids, it was normal to experience noise and traffic in and out of the front door, but this was different. Something was wrong.

"Didn't you hear what I said? There's a fire in your garage. You need to get out now!"

Finally, I understood. Seconds passed, but it seemed like minutes. I jumped up, looked at her, and then back to the garage door. There was no sign of smoke or smell, but obviously something had caused a stranger to barge into my home.

I quickly ran to the back door and slammed it open. Running quickly across the patio I rounded the house and headed toward the front garage. Almost immediately I saw smoke, lots of smoke. A huge black plume reached into the sky hundreds of feet into the air. I now smelled the acrid smoke of plastic and rubber from our city garbage containers that were melted into a messy ball of trash. The redwood fence and gate spewed flames that reached eight to nine feet high. Then I saw a shadow through the smoke.

A Hispanic man I didn't know held a water hose connected to the side of the house. The water gushed onto the doorframe of the garage and the front gate. He yelled, "Get another hose! Quick!"

I sprinted to the backyard and grabbed the longest hose we owned and attached it to a hose bib. Luckily, Joan and I were gardeners and hoses were located at every outdoor faucet. I then quickly turned the spigot. Water sprayed into my face and onto my shirt as the hose twisted like I had grabbed an angry snake.

I don't remember getting to the fire erupting from the door jam and side eaves of the roof. I do remember spraying the fire in a wild attempt to stop the flames and beat back the nasty smelling smoke as it bellowed out from the garage door. The concept of time disappeared as we desperately sprayed and hosed the wall and roof line.

Sometime during the furious action of trying to save our home, Rick Dorris, the city fire chief, appeared out of the swirling chaos and stood next to me. I emphatically greeted him with approval. "Boy, am I glad to see you!"

Rick threw water, but it wasn't what I expected. "Keep hosing it down. Our fire units are tied up with another fire across town. Another unit is being readied and will be here as soon as we can get it out of the station." I liked Rick. We had joined the Dixon Lions Club at the same time. He had been seriously injured when he was a young fireman and walked with a noticeable limp but had used grit, determination, and a gregarious personality to rise through the ranks to become the local chief. But I wasn't sure I liked Rick at that moment.

Finally, a fire engine and several firefighters arrived. I still have no recollection of how long the event lasted, but I was exhausted. The professionals brought in large hoses and equipment enabling them to enter the garage and beat down all flames until they were extinguished. Compared to what might have happened, the damage was light and our insurance paid the $20,000 worth of repair work. Turned out I had caused the fire. I'd poured three-day-old used briquets out of the barbecue into the city garbage container. Something caught fire inside, incinerating the rubber, and then jumped to the house.

When I looked around to thank the two people responsible for helping me at a time of need, they were gone. Someone told me later that parents at the soccer game two blocks away saw the large black plume, which was easily spotted from the C. A. Jacobs School soccer field. Thankfully two citizens took the time to help when they saw a need. Years later I met the young lady when she introduced herself at a school function where I was principal. I gave her a belated thank you and made sure she knew how much I appreciated her actions helping a stranger. In fact, I thanked her every time I saw her and still do 20 years later. Do Americans help out strangers more often than citizens of other countries? I like to think that empathy and a concern for others is part of our character.

Chapter 41

THE PARENT MURDER

"Mr. Rott, the police called and want you to call them. It's an emergency." I was in the courtyard where students ate lunch most days of the year. Large, heavy-duty picnic tables dotted the space in a square protected by mature deciduous trees, which shaded students from the sun in the warmer months of April to October. In cooler weather, students ate in the multipurpose room. As school principal, I chose to spend the three lunch periods assisting our monitors and school custodians. I helped with all duties needing attention, especially interacting with students. The time was routine but important for the smooth transition into the next block of afternoon learning time while giving teachers a lunch break. I expected this day to be like thousands of other routine days I spent on duty. I was wrong.

I looked up to see Xochilt Quitegua, our office manager as I was tearing the foil wrapper off a container of yogurt. Her face flashed "problem." I had hired Xochilt several years earlier. I teased her by telling her that I hired her because I loved her name, which was as odd as mine. Quickly, she became indispensable to the school.

She lowered her voice. "Mr. Rott, the police just called and said that Belinda Lucas was shot and killed less than an hour ago."

We knew Belinda Lucas well. Her two boys had attended our school for several years. Belinda lived a hard life but was trying to make a better one for her sons. She dropped them off every morning and picked them up near the school office at the end of the day. She frequently stopped by the office to say hello or to gossip with other parents or school staff. Tattoos were visible on her arms and the back of her neck. She was ahead of the curve as most of our parents were not wearing tattoos at that time. She had left her husband because he abused her, and he was known around town as a troubled young man with a bad disposition.

"What did they say? What happened?' I said, trying to control the volume of my voice.

"That's all they said except they want you to call this number." She passed me a yellow sticky note with a phone number. I walked quickly to the administration building and then into my office where I closed the door.

"This is Mr. Rott, Principal of Tremont School."

"Mr. Rott, this is Sergeant Phillips. We need to inform you that Mrs. Belinda Lucas was shot while walking her dogs this morning. An investigation is ongoing."

"I understand." I didn't, but I said I did anyway.

"Are the Lucas boys at school?" he asked.

"Yeah, I think so. I saw Belinda this morning and I'm pretty sure both boys were with her."

"I'm going to have someone call you soon and give you instructions concerning the boys," he said and he hung up.

As I left my office, I told Xochilt not to repeat what we knew. "We don't want to start any rumors or create unnecessary speculation without further direction from the district office or the police." I called the district office and was instructed by the superintendent to follow the directions of the police department.

The last lunch bell rang ending recess, and I started walking from the playground to the office. Xochilt met me halfway and said I needed to call Child Protective Services. I took the second sticky note of the day and immediately called the number.

"This is Mr. Rott from Tremont School in Dixon. I was asked to call this number." I told the CPS worker that the boys were still at school, and I didn't have any information about how they were getting home.

The CPS worker left me with this sobering instruction: "Arrangements will be made for the boys and we'll be there before school ends. Whatever happens, don't let them leave with their father." He hung up. *Oh, brother,* I thought.

The next hour and a half felt like the longest 90 minutes ever. I didn't eat the sandwich and apple sitting in the school refrigerator. I waited for someone to arrive. No police car or white Ford Fairlane, used by county employees, drove to the front of the school." *Now what?* I thought. *What's going on?*

The end-of-school horn blared with a personal and ominous message that only I heard. Smiling parents walked forward to meet jumping and twirling students. Small bodies rushed past glad the school day had ended. A lone whistle blew to warn a student to stop running through the crowded courtyard to the school exit. Then I saw him.

Jess Lucas was walking my way with a scowl and determination. He held each boy by their arms as if they were calves on their way to branding. *What should I do?* I walked toward Jess and the frightened boys.

"Are you alright?" tumbled out of my mouth.

Jess shot me an angry look. "What do you think? My boys' mother is dead." His voice ramped higher as he spit out the ugly words.

"Let me know what we can do. We're here for the boys." I barely recognized my voice. Why I made that choice I don't know. I silently walked with Jess and the boys to the curb and watched them get into his car. No police were in sight. *They must know he is picking up the boys.*

The next morning, I read in the newspaper that the authorities had arrested a couple from Vallejo for murder. The man and woman started in Vallejo in a methamphetamine-soaked journey. A 30-mile crime spree resulted in several shootings, culminating in the murder of a Dixon woman neither knew. Belinda had died a random victim of a drug-fueled psychosis and crime spree.

No one from law enforcement or CPS ever contacted me concerning the horrific event. Eventually, CPS placed the boys with relatives living in Oregon. I've thought about that day hundreds of times and have so many questions. Did I do the right thing? Why didn't I confront the father as instructed by CPS? Today, under the same circumstances, a schoolwide lockdown with a police presence is the probable response. Ironically, that's not progress.

WHAT HAPPENED ALONG THE WAY

Chapter 42

THE NUMBER 24 TRAM

"Where are we?" I muttered in a soft voice. A silence startled us as we both looked up.

"I thought you knew. Weren't you paying attention? This isn't the city crafts' fair." Joan replied, her voice heavy with annoyance and a pinch of disgust.

A few seconds earlier, Joan sat reading the summary of the next day's guided tour while reviewing maps with points of interest highlighted as we trundled down the tracks. I spent my time gazing out the window. Now we were the only passengers on the tram and it wasn't moving.

"Well, yeah," I replied immediately. I checked and rechecked the directions before we decided to use the mass transit system on our own. We found the tram we were looking for, the number 24, and boarded.

Now the Number 24 Amsterdam tram had stopped. I looked in all directions, and we appeared to be in the middle of a large maintenance yard fenced in on three sides by a ten-foot wire metal fence.

Two men dressed identically in black pants, white shirts, and black vests stepped down from the conductor's section in the front of the tram. Each was carrying what that looked like metal lunch boxes. They slowly walked toward a metal building at the edge of the fence line.

I decided to take action. Leaving Joan still seated, I rose from my seat and ran quickly for the open door. I yelled, "Excuse me. Do you speak English?"

"Of course," replied the taller of the two men. His face showed no expression.

"I guess we're lost. My wife and I wanted to attend the Saturday Crafts Fair, but we must have missed the stop." He shook his head slightly as if he understood the implications but offered nothing more.

"We need to get back to the City Central. I think we're lost. What should we do?"

I saw no busy streets or traffic. We seemed to be in an industrial zone of some kind. There were no taxis or transportation systems in sight.

Finally, he replied in perfect English, "We are going to eat. In thirty minutes, a train will leave here going back where you started. It will be the 24 Line. Get on. You'll have to wait until then." He turned and continued walking and disappeared with his partner into a small building with Dutch words printed over the door.

"I thought you were paying attention," Joan said, an unhappy look on her face. "How long were we riding with no one else on board?" she asked.

"I guess I was tired or something and zoned out." I felt terrible. We only had a day in Amsterdam and this little adventure was going to cost us the major part of the afternoon. I was going to say we'd be back again someday but thought better of it.

A standing family joke was that I possessed no sense of direction. None. I don't know if growing up in a small town contributed to this inability to successfully navigate with or without a map.

Joan, on the other hand, quickly assumed the job of family navigator. She excelled in getting us to our destination whether it was in a city like San Francisco, Portland, or Sacramento or in the mountains of California and Oregon. Early in our marriage, we squabbled occasionally about which direction to take, but that soon ended when it became apparent that if we wanted to get to our destination, Joan's directions worked.

Later, reconnecting with people on our tour, it became clear that the Number 24 Tram was the correct tram to take to the crafts' fair. Did we go the wrong way or miss our stop? I don't know. That evening we were both able to laugh at our day's misadventure. We discovered on our trips that one of the joys of traveling are the misadventures, and like *a dish best eaten cold,* you often enjoy the experience at a later time. The Number 24 Tram story has been shared with family and friends. I'm sure more stories are just around the next trip.

Chapter 43

THE SUDDEN ATTACK

For many years, Joan and I rented a house on the Northern California coast for Labor Day to gather our children and enjoy time near the ocean. We spent many summer vacation weeks renting a house in Trinidad, north of Eureka. We spent long days walking the beach with our dogs as well as exploring the coast looking for agates, petrified wood, and jasper. The first few years we stayed in campgrounds on the north coast which was fun and inexpensive. Later we decided to rent houses with real beds. We all looked forward to this time together. On September 6, 2016, I almost didn't make it home.

One day earlier, we arrived in Trinidad and moved into a large house overlooking the quaint fishing harbor. We were ready to hit the beach and ocean to begin our relaxing vacation routine. Erik and his wife, Katie, brought their daughter, Hattie, our first grandchild, as well as Indie, the largest brown Labrador retriever I have ever seen. He kept our Standard Schnauzer, Sadie, company. Also present were Ivan and Sammy, then living in Oregon, and Tara, who was living in Mendocino County.

On our first morning everyone but Joan and me went fishing. Joan watched Hattie, and I explored Trinidad with the dogs. September is the best time of year for visiting the California coast and the sun shone most of the day. There was not a hint of fog or overhead clouds. The fishing crew returned with a near limit of ling and rock cod. The fish were quickly filleted and bagged to be frozen for later. That night's dinner included fresh fish and home-grown summer tomatoes balanced with delicious north coast wine.

The next day started much like the day before except for the focus on hunting rocks. Our group headed for the beach and started looking for semi-precious stones. Everyone found small numbers, although Ivan found the largest number: 14 white-banded agates and two red speckled jasper, all smoothed by sea and sand. Back at the rental, we did our routine of displaying our stones on a table to be compared and enjoyed by all present.

Ivan and I decided to take Indie and Sadie for a walk to the beach. After a short distance, I found myself suddenly out of breath. I bent over and complained to Ivan, "Man, I'm really out of shape. Just a minute and let me catch my breath." At the same time, my chest felt odd and there was a pressure that I had never experienced, even when playing sports like basketball and football. I prided myself on staying in shape. I played city league basketball into my 40s and hiked regularly with a group from Woodland. A month earlier, we hiked to the top of Mount Tamalpais. After a minute or two, I told Ivan I wanted to go back to the house and rest.

I quickly felt better and absorbed the good-natured barbs of everyone as we laughed about Dad slowing down. "Maybe you should stay and watch Hattie for the remainder of the trip," Erik laughed. "Admit it, you can't keep up."

"I can keep up with you any day," I scoffed.

The next day was unscheduled and everyone slept in and lounged around the house reading or catching sun on the porch. I decided I would walk Indie and Sadie as I had done dozens of times on our trips. They were always anxious to check out the *flora and fauna* along the beach trail. Soon after we left the property, I became overwhelmed with breathlessness and a stronger chest pressure than the day before. I realized that something was wrong.

After returning to the house, I found Erik, Katie, and Hattie napping on a blanket on the living room floor. I shook Erik. "Hey, I think I need to go to the hospital." Erik slowly opened one eye, then the other shot open.

At a small hospital in Arcata, I was examined and questioned by staff. "Do you smoke? Any problems or issues with cholesterol, family diabetes, or heart problems?"

I explained that I had been in good health but my father had died of a heart attack when he was 75. An older doctor came in to talk with me. He put me at ease after a few minutes and explained that results from their tests were inconclusive. He recommended seeing my doctor when I returned home as I might be showing signs of *unstable angina*. He would provide the supporting data they had collected for me to take home.

"That doesn't sound too bad," I told Erik on the way home. "I've heard of angina but don't know too much about it. Chest pains or something. I'll get it checked out when we get home."

I was sitting at the patio discussing the situation with the family when Katie, who is a nurse, asked what the paperwork said. I found the packet and started reading a lot of legal, bureaucratic words, and then something caught our attention. In big bold letters in the middle of one page, I signed, it said, **"After being advised not to leave the hospital, you insisted on leaving our care to seek medical support from your doctor."**

"What the heck?" I almost shouted. I quickly emailed my doctor but since I am a Kaiser patient, I didn't know when I would hear back.

Surprisingly, I received an email that evening. My doctor's message said something like, "What are you doing out and about with unstable angina? Get to our offices or to a hospital immediately!"

After two ambulance rides, stops at four hospitals, and a surgical implantation of three heart stents, I finally arrived home with new insight. Evidently, I had dodged a full-blown heart attack. I also discovered that ambulance beds are built for people who are six feet or shorter. I learned that new anesthesia allows a patient to be weirdly awake and "out" at the same time. During the procedure to place stents, doctors really do talk about where they have been for dinner recently and where they are having lunch while next asking for a clamp and a sponge. Most importantly, I understand that angina can be serious and at hospitals it's best to read all paperwork you sign. Today I'm 20 pounds lighter, carry heart medicine at all times, and eat a more balanced diet. I didn't think it possible, but I value family trips even more than before. Still no one imagined what lay ahead two short years later.

Chapter 44

THE WEIRD SNIFF HOTEL

"Hey, Dad," Ivan said, "did you notice the building across the street?"

I saw a new four-story building with two floors of glass windows. Behind the windows on the back walls were long banks of television sets. They were all on. There was movement near the windows, but I couldn't make out what I was seeing.

"Yeah. What's that all about?"

People in Portland like to brag about how their city is weird. In fact, there are signs placed around town that reading "**Keep Portland Weird.**" Ivan and Sammy claim the signs are placed by the City of Portland, but I haven't figured out whether they are yanking my chain or not. With famous locations and points of interest like Voodoo Donuts, I'm inclined to believe them, and I've come to think that anything is possible.

"You want to have a look?" he asked.

"Sure. I'm game," I replied.

Light rain hung in the air in typical Northwest fashion as Ivan and I crossed the street. We walked quickly. He smiled as we entered a lobby. I ran my eyes over a large interior with smooth stone floors and a simple hotel chandelier. On the left were two young people dressed in grey vests over white shirts and black bowties who were working behind a large counter. One looked up and smiled while the other scanned a computer screen and used the keyboard to input unseen data.

"What is this place, Ivan? I don't see anything special here." So far this seemed to me a rather boring side trip. Ivan is cerebral and is often reading at all times of the day and night. I never know what to expect when I am with him.

"Just wait," he said. "Let's walk down the lobby." We rounded a curved section and I saw a bar with the kind of stools that invite people to sit and drink, day and night. Three or four beer spigots were placed for easy access by a bartender pouring draft beer. But instead of back counters with expensive hard liquors, liqueurs and wines, the space was open and a large area of artificial grass was visible behind the bartender.

"You have got to be kidding," I blurted out, and then I started laughing and shaking my head.

Running and playing together were at least six dogs. Dog toys were scattered throughout the space and two young black Labradors were playing keep away with a large red rubber bone. A couple sat at the end of the bar drinking beer.

"Welcome to the Sniff Hotel," Ivan snickered. "Dogs are boarded here when their owners are on vacation or business trips. The feature I like best is the daycare for dogs' option. At the end of the day, owners pick up their pets and have a drink or two watching them as they romp and play. Owners relax and unwind after a tough day at work." On both sides of the bar were signs. The one on the left was a chalk board that announced *Yappy Hour Specials* and a list of brews carefully printed in colored chalk. On the other was a permanent sign that said, *60 Minute Doggie Massages*. I thought about the plain kennel where we boarded Sadie and how the "expensive" $20 a day fee caused me to grimace. We thought a rural Dixon kennel an outrageous extravagance.

As we left, Ivan took me to the opposite side of the building where I looked up to see the nicely placed sign, **Sniff Hotel,** on an outside wall. The bank of windows I had earlier were TV sets in the dogs' rooms to keep them company. A brochure for the hotel also described the wading pool on the top floor.

All this made me think about three things: First, Americans love their pets. Next, if a dog hotel doesn't bark income inequality, I don't know what does. Finally, Portland is weird.

Chapter 45

THE RETURN TO HUNSPACH

The words of the ship's tour director rang harsh and unforgiving in my ears. "You must be back by 5:00 pm or we will leave without you. The Captain says you will then have to meet us at our next stop in Heidelberg. We're on a strict schedule with no exceptions."

The phone clicked off. My call to plead our case, as we rushed back, was not successful. I remember catching a short glimpse of the German captain of our Viking Cruise once. He quickly skirted our group as it was lined up to leave for the day's morning onshore tour at eight. Tall, well dressed in a white uniform and with stern expression, he nodded in our direction. As we now raced through the Alsatian countryside, I thought, *Why didn't we get an easy-going Danish or Norwegian captain?*

My German cousin Brigitte met us on a September day in 2015 after the morning tour to Strasbourg. Our afternoons were typically free time to explore on our own. I was thrilled to meet a distant Rott cousin thanks to the Internet and they drove us to our ancestral Alsatian village of Hunspach.

"Hello, are you Brigitte?" I asked tentatively. A man and two women sat at a table in a park on the French side next to the Rhine River where the ship was moored for the day.

"Yes, yes. You're Dan. This is my husband, Rudi Feyh, and my mother, Annmarie Rott," one of the women said. After a few minutes to introduce Joan and engage in small talk, we understood that Rudi and Annmarie spoke no English but Brigitte spoke four European languages and would translate. We walked to the car, Brigitte telling me that Rudi had helped build the car they were driving. He had worked for Mercedes in Stuttgart for over 40 years. Waiting for us was a large white Mercedes.

I said, "We need to return before 5 so the captain doesn't leave us behind." We all laughed and got in. The street was lined with tall ash type trees that provided perfect shade for the houses on the French side of the street overlooking the Rhine. A street repair crew sat next to a large trench with sections of decomposing pipe torn out minutes before. I can't remember what they were eating, but I did notice that next to each man was a large liter bottle of beer. This is very much part of the European culture but I am always a bit shocked and raise my eyebrows when I see construction workers drinking beer on a job site.

Our family left Hunspach in 1809 to emigrate to Russia at the urging of Catherine the Great, herself a German, who had married the czar. She was convinced that Germans were better educated and better trained to farm and build than native Russians. The southern area of Russia had been cleared of Turks and other nomadic peoples and promised to be the "bread basket" of Russia if it were properly developed. Czarina Catherine hoped that our ancestors would use their talents to develop farming areas to rival anything found in Western Europe. She devised a list of incentives to attract German settlers. In 1870 when those incentives, such as religious freedom and no military service, were overturned, many German Russians headed back to Germany or left for the Americas. My great-grandfather's family left in 1889.

"Oh, Dan, you will love our village. It is so beautiful," Brigitte said.

"But isn't it in France?" I interjected. "We're ethnic Germans. Why are our ancestors from France?"

"Oh, Dan. You have so much to learn about Europe. These are border lands and have changed control many times. This area of Alsace is mostly ethnic German."

We turned off the main highway and passed several small

villages that reminded me of a miniature Colmar or Strasbourg with buildings of black half-timbers crisscrossing white stucco walls.

"Look at the windows. German and French aren't the only divisions here. Do you see the drapes in the windows?" Brigitte explained that religious differences were also historically present in the Alsace. Catholics hung red drapes while Protestants fashioned blue ones although most religious differences were now reconciled.

I kept looking at my watch. The trip only took 45 minutes. We reached our destination in a timely manner, but I'm always nervous where time and timelines are concerned. The village was very small, but each house was beautifully maintained in the Alsatian tradition. Individual houses alternated between dark orange or charcoal tiled roofs. Many windows were lined with flower boxes overflowing with colorful nasturtiums. Narrow streets served as sidewalks and butted up to the houses leaving no room for front yards or ground level landscaping of any kind. The houses, roofs, and flower boxes provided an assortment of rich color and a sense of welcoming.

We saw very few people on the streets as we took photos and walked to the cemetery. We passed the small, plain but attractive white Protestant church. Hunspach is still a Protestant village. Beautiful and intricately carved headstones pushed up through the grass. There were many Rott markers.

"Until recently many Rotts still lived here but over the years young people have moved on to find good jobs in the cities." Brigitte explained. "There is only one Rott family left and they are elderly. On our last visit, we talked to them for a short time. They didn't seem too interested in speaking with relatives whose families left 200 years before."

We ended a perfect day having a lunch Brigitte arranged with the owner of a bed and breakfast. The building was erected by one of our ancestors in 1730. The name B H Rott is carved into the main door frame and is still visible. We said our goodbyes, took a last photo, and Rudi eased the white Mercedes back to the highway. A perfect day ended there. Until somehow Rudi made a wrong turn.

After making several stops to ask directions using Brigitte's French, we pulled up to the riverside park in fear and apprehension. It was 4:58 and we heard the low rumble of the river boat's engines. We yelled, "Good-bye," and sprinted toward the Rhine. Smoke and river water boiled and mixed at the back of the boat. Then I saw them; boat lines still holding our Viking home tight to the pier. We ran up the gangplank, heads down, not making eye contact, but feeling wonderful about our accomplishment. Another Rott returned to Hunspach.

Chapter 46

THE SADDEST CLOUDS

"Ahh, humph. Hoof, Ohhh, man."

"Dan, are you alright?" Joan was almost shouting.

Sammy followed up quickly with, "What happened?"

At almost the same time, I heard Ivan say, "Dad? Dad!" I still hadn't opened my eyes. I lay on my side on the pavement in the parking lot of the Elevester Hotel in Norway's Jotunheiman Mountains National Park. It was September 2018 and we had stopped for the night in the old-style hotel recommended in Rick Steves' travel guide to Norway.

Our first night had been spent at Aud's home in Hernes with her second husband, Geir.

"Dad? Dad? Can you sit up?" asked Ivan. He's a physical therapist, and I felt his practiced hands cupping my shoulder. I didn't move an inch. The air pushed partially out of my lungs. My ribs and lower shoulder stung with pain. After catching my breath, I opened my eyes to see Joan and Sammy kneeling next to me with worry etched on their faces.

After wrenching myself up with Ivan's help, I determined that nothing was broken and I was ready to push on. My left side was sore but there didn't appear to be any real damage. "What did you do? I'm not sure you should go with us on the hike," Joan counseled. "That was terrible. I heard you hit the ground. Maybe something is wrong and caused you to fall."

"No, no. That's not it. I put my foot up to the top of that wooden pallet leaning on the outbuilding and the bottom of my shoe got caught on one of the wooden slats. I lost my balance and couldn't dislodge the shoe tread." I fell like a redwood tree without any ability to soften the fall. "I'm good. Let's go," I insisted. "After coming this distance with my family, I'm not stopping now. I'm fine." I felt embarrassed for what I referred to in the past as an old man's accident.

The others made faces and shook their heads but with no further delays, we struck off for the trail. Hiking with my family was an experience of a lifetime and I intended to fill my days exploring the land of my ancestors with them. The first half of that trip turned out to be one of the best experiences of my life. There was no indication of what lay ahead on the trip.

At the trailhead, we found wooden hiking sticks kindly left by other travelers and began the ascent into the higher elevations. We saw raw beauty in almost every direction beginning at the narrow valley floor. Thin, soft clouds hung nearby as if silently tracking the glaciers. In some ways I thought them the most beautiful clouds I'd ever seen. Joan and I took photos trying to capture their simple elegance. For the first hour we experienced a moderate climb. Except for the highest elevations, I noticed the trees were not typical evergreens found in most West Coast mountains but small, strong trees stunted from their fight with brutal winter weather.

Then Ivan and I heard Sammy and Joan yell for us. We turned around to see them bending down taking photos of something we had missed as we talked and watched the mountain peaks become larger and clearer with our approach. As we backtracked, we noticed gorgeous shiny red and peach mushrooms. I had always thought they were a creative product of artists and cartoonists. Joan and Sammy both had huge grins and expressive eyes as they examined the shiny colored caps with bright white polka dotted accents. My cousin, Steiner, told me later that Vikings used the mushrooms before going into battle but his big smile gave him away as a tease.

The trail snaked up the rocky, granite ridgelines wet with trickles of water flowing downhill after melting from glaciers crouching between mountain crests. Eventually the trickles merged with mountain streams as their journey hurried on uninterrupted to the iconic Scandinavian fjords and finally the North Sea.

"I'm glad these mountains are rocky. Otherwise we'd be slogging in mud and muck up to our ankles," Ivan said as we neared the large glacier above.

As we encountered larger rocks and shiny black outcroppings, Joan's ankles and one knee started to ache from an old injury. My ribs were still sore from the fall. "Why don't you two go ahead and see if you can reach the glacier? Mom and I will take more photos here and rest up our aches and pains." I encouraged Ivan and Sammy forward. Joan and I were holding them back, and they were determined to reach ice. And that is what they did.

Three days later we said our goodbyes to Ivan and Sammy at the Oslo airport and then we waited for our midday flight and tour from Berlin to Prague and then Vienna. Joan and I reminisced about what we had experienced from crossing fjords to getting a tour of the old family homestead. We laughed and made faces remembering the boiled sheep and cabbage dish, a Norwegian delicacy, proudly served by a cousin and his wife. We looked forward to barbecued California tri-tip. At some point, Joan looked over and said, "When we get home, you're going to get a complete physical." I turned away and rolled my eyes and gently shook my head.

A little over a week later, I sat alone on the plane leaving Vienna. After a vicious, ironic twist of fate and a surprise massive heart attack that hit Joan out of nowhere, I was beginning a new life without my partner of forty years. Feeling hollowed out and exhausted, I stared straight ahead as clouds moved quickly past the airplane windows.

Made in the USA
Coppell, TX
13 July 2020